VIA Folios 59

Autobiographical Poems

FRANCESCA TURINI BUFALINI

Autobiographical Poems
A Bilingual Edition

Edited by
NATALIA COSTA-ZALESSOW

Translations by
JOAN E. BORRELLI
with the participation of
Natalia Costa-Zalessow

BORDIGHERA PRESS

Library of Congress Control Number: 2009908625

Printed in the United States.

Published by
BORDIGHERA PRESS
John D. Calandra Italian American Institute
25 W. 43rd Street, 17th Floor
New York, NY 10036

VIA FOLIOS 59
ISBN 978–1–59954–009–2

ACKNOWLEDGMENTS

My special thanks go to Joan E. Borrelli, my translator, former student and now friend, for her moral support, prodding, and encouragement to finish this book, which I had practically given up during my long illness. I also thank her for her dedication in rereading the manuscript and checking it for typographical errors.

I am grateful to Giovanna Maria Pucci, librarian of the Biblioteca Comunale San Giustino, for providing me with a copy of Milani and Bà's book, with other articles on Francesca Turini Bufalini, and for her help in obtaining the images included in this book.

I also thank Professor Dino S. Cervigni for looking up Turini Bufalini's poems in Guaccimani's anthology, *Raccolta di sonetti d'autori diversi et eccellenti dell'età nostra,* located in the Rare Book section of the library of the University of North Carolina at Chapel Hill.

IMAGES

The illustrations in this book are courtesy of the *Comune di Città di Castello* (Municipality of Città di Castello) and the *Ministero per i Beni e le Attività Culturali — Direzione Regionale per i Beni Culturali e Paesaggistici dell'Umbria — Soprintendenza per i Beni Storici, Artistici ed Etnoantropologici Perugia; San Giustino* (Ministry of Cultural Properties and Activities — Regional Administration of Cultural and Scenic Properties of Umbria — Management for Historic, Artistic and Ethno-anthropological Properties, Perugia and San Giustino). Our gratitude to:

Dr. Anna Maria Traversini, Biblioteca Comunale "Giosuè Carducci," Città di Castello

Arch. Benedetta Rossi, Office of Properties — Sport Facilities, Municipality of Città di Castello

Dr. Giuditta Rossi, Management for Historic, Artistic and Ethno-anthropological Properties, Perugia

Dr. Vilma Cioci, Cultural Services, Municipality of San Giustino

David Domini, Data and Reproduction Center, Municipality of San Giustino

BOOK COVER: Portrait of Francesca Turini Bufalini, preserved in the Bufalini Palace, Città di Castello (photo: Studio Ballini, Città di Castello), reproduced against the background of the palace's portico.

CONTENTS

INTRODUCTION

In her *Rime* (1627–28), Francesca Turini Bufalini included a series of sonnets under the subtitle "Principio dello stato dell'autrice" [Beginning of the author's life]. These poems are unique for their truly autobiographical nature, openly declared as such by the author herself. None of the European women poets preceding her, or any of her contemporaries, recorded their lives with such precision. In these sonnets, Turini Bufalini gives us a detailed description of her life, from childhood to old age, along with the full spectrum of her emotions. She describes her birth followed by the death of her father and mother, her lonely, rustic but free life as an orphan in her uncle's castle in the wilderness of the Apennines (where she kept company with shepherdesses, rode horses and went hunting), her marriage, her exuberant joys of motherhood, her sad widowhood, love for her children and grandchildren, trouble with her adult sons and the tragic death of one of them. In most poems a strong, narrating "I" predominates, but frequently the author also addresses herself, her heart and her soul in the personal "you" voice.

Many themes in Turini Bufalini's autobiographical poems are the first of their kind in the Western poetic canon. Such personal subject matter, and the intimacy of its presentation, does not reemerge in Western literature until much later. With Turini Bufalini's poetry, the themes of past youthful emotions, of childbirth and miscarriage, of motherhood and the raising of children are introduced into Italian literature. Moreover, in weaving her personal struggle into her poetic invention and in sharing the intimate details of her daily life, her poetry exceeds in originality that of other European women poets of her time, regardless of nationality. These characteristics make Turini Bufalini seem closer to the Romantic tendency towards personal confession, rather than to the literary stylization of her own age. And yet, during her own time and throughout the centuries, she has received little credit for her thematic innovations. Along with seventeenth-century Italian literature, she was for many centuries forgotten, and has been only recently rediscovered as a writer. Her life has currently been reconstructed on the basis of documents preserved in various archives, including the Bufalini Family Archives at San Giustino — documents which attest that her poems may indeed be accepted as autobiographical. Still lacking, however, is a study of her contribution to Italian literature, a lacuna which I hope to bridge with this volume.

With my introduction and notes, and my selection of what I consider to be Turini Bufalini's best poems, I point out the parallelism between events in her actual life and her poetic compositions. I examine her style, themes and quality as a poet who wrote on subjects not seen before in the works of other women poets. Where possible, I compare her verses to those of Italian poets preceding her. I also review and comment on the opinions of literary critics regarding her work.

★★★★★

According to recently found baptismal records,[1] Francesca Porzia was born on July 23, 1553, in Borgo Sansepolcro, a town in Tuscany, close to Umbria. Her father, Giovanni Turini (also spelled Turrini and Torrino), was a professional soldier who, as a youth, had joined the troops of Giovanni de' Medici (known as Giovanni delle Bande Nere). Turini became famous for a duel with a companion-in-arms, Amico da Venafro, imposed on the two by their strict and violent commander for having quarreled with each other. When both collapsed from their wounds, Giovanni had them swear eternal friendship. After Giovanni's death (Nov. 1526), Turini participated with other members of the Bande Nere in the short-lived defense of the Florentine Republic. He then joined the group of exiles, under the leadership of Pietro Strozzi, in service to France.[2] Turini distinguished himself first in the service of the French king, Francis I, from whom he received, in 1543, rights to the castle at Stupinigi (Piedmont), and again in the service of Henry II,[3] who

---

[1] Now preserved at "Archivio Comunale Sansepolcro."

[2] See Ricotti 44, 47, 58–59, 76, 83.

[3] During the sixteenth century, the Italian peninsula was divided into several independent states, at continual war with each other. Moreover, the region was the battlefield of the two major European powers of the time — France and Spain — a situation which forced the Italians to eventually take up arms with one side or the other. The Du Bellay brothers mention Turini, their contemporary, several times in their *Mémoires* (Vol. 3: 42, 223, 326, 336, 415, 419, and 422) under the French spelling of his name, Jean de Turin, as a *"capitaine"* in charge of 500 Italian soldiers in 1536, and in 1537 of 1000 Italians protecting Savigliano (Savillan in French) during the struggle in Piedmont between the French and Spanish armies. From the *Catalogue des Actes de François Ier* (vol. 6: 617, #22107; vol. 8: 692, #32890; vol. 6: 729, #22707; and vol. 4: 623, #13911) we learn that Turini (Jean Torino also Thurin) was granted permission, in Feb. 1540, to live in the Stupinigi Castle, was ennobled in May 1540, and, in Dec. 1543, was given ownership, for the duration of his life, of the Stupinigi Castle. In May 1544, he was granted French citizenship, together with his first wife. In the *Catalogue des Actes de François Ier*, Turini is referred to as *"capitaine de*

renewed the rights in 1547. Confusion remains concerning Giovanni Turini's life and details of the lives of his sons, and their achievements as military men; nor is it clear which of his sons belong to his first marriage to Diamante de' Bernardini, who is mentioned by name in the French document of 1544. However, sometime after 1544, Giovanni Turini married Count Francesco Carpegna's daughter, Camilla, who had been raised at the refined court of the dukes of Urbino.[4] He died in late 1553, not 1554, in Corsica (during the French invasion of the island begun in August 1553), while assisting his commander, Paul de La Barthe, *Seigneur* de Thermes (also spelled Termes), to supply the town of San Fiorenzo, besieged by the imperial troops of Andrea Doria, to whom it was subsequently surrendered in 1554. He was killed by friendly fire, struck by a stray shot from the rifle of one of his soldiers during a skirmish with the enemy.[5] He was still remembered in the nineteenth century, for his portrait appeared among the seven miniature medallions of Borgo Sansepolcro's most illustrious men, depicted on the first inner page of the handwritten album offered by the city of Sansepolcro on June 21, 1883, to the memory of Garibaldi, *Album d'onore offerto dalla città di Sansepolcro il 2 giugno 1883 alla memoria di Giuseppe Garibaldi*, now on view in Rome at the Museo del Risorgimento (MCRR. Ms. 830). The medallions were painted by Ettore Sampaolo. Turini's face corresponds to that of his full-length portrait still preserved in Borgo Sansepolcro (in Sala Consiliare).[6]

Turini's oldest son, Girolamo, born c. 1531 (and therefore from Turini's first wife), succeeded in obtaining, in 1553, his father's position and pension, and served under Admiral Gaspard de Coligny and Maréchal Henri de Montmorency. Girolamo later became "gentilhomme de la chambre du roi," and

---

gents de pied" [foot-soldiers]. In the 1547 document granted by Henry II, Turini is referred to as "*présentement colonel de deux bandes italiennes au Piémont*," *Catalogue des Actes de Henry II* (vol. 1: 306, #09.233), and he is still "*colonel*" in 1552 (vol. 7: 269, #11859). Nowhere is there a mention of a title such as "count, *seigneur*, or *maréchal*" as given by Mercati ("Cenni storici..." 19) and by Milani (see Milani and Bà 12). Francesca, in her *Rime sacre*, referred to her father as "*capitano*." See note 39.

[4]The Carpegna family of the Scavolino branch had a common ancestry with the Montefeltro, dukes of Urbino (see Torrioli 5, col. 1). Camilla is listed among the fourteen children of Francesco Carpegna (1478–1553) and his wife, Francesca Ottoni di Matelica (1490–1529). No birth date is given for her. It is stated that she married Giovanni Turini, but no date is recorded. See Carpegna Falconieri 128.

[5]"... *scaramucciando ambe le parti inavvedutamente da uno de'suoi soldati, fu ucciso con colpo di fucile Giovanni da Torino bravo e vecchio Capitano*" (Limperani 398).

[6]A reproduction of Turini's portrait, unfortunately of poor quality, appears in Milani and Bà's book (18).

died in 1567 during the battle of Saint-Denis.[7] Turini fathered two other sons, Andrea and Arduino, and three daughters. The oldest girl, Giulia, married Count Monteauto; the second, Livia, entered a convent in Borgo Sansepolcro and became a nun.

Francesca was the youngest of the Turini siblings. Soon after her father's death, she lost her mother, as well, and was brought up by her maternal uncle, Count Pietro Carpegna, in his castle of Gattara (now only a ruin), in Tuscany, situated close to the border of Montefeltro, surrounded by the wilderness of the Apennines. In poem **1** (the references set in bold type are poem numbers referring to the present volume) she recalls her father's death and how she and her mother were given a home by her uncle. The rustic, wild ambience of Gattara, with its solitude, forests, and pastoral setting, is repeatedly depicted throughout the poems in which she describes her youth (Part I).

Francesca laments that she did not receive a proper education (**2–3**), which would have prepared her for writing poetry; instead she was given a spindle and a needle,[8] leaving her handicapped as a writer for the rest of her life (**3**). But she was granted a lot of freedom and became quite a sportswoman. She roamed the valleys with the local shepherdesses, watched the sheep graze and observed them being milked (**2**). She sang and made music with these rustic girls (**6** and **7**). She competed with them in running and frequently won (**11**). But even when alone, she was close to nature, whether picking flowers or washing her face and bosom in the cold water of the brooks (**5**). Accompanied by a hound, she went hunting, with bow and arrow, or fishing and bird-catching (**12**). She was also an able rider and took her horse up steep hills for the thrill it brought her while toying with danger (**10**). All of these subjects appear for the first time in Italian women's poetry and are, moreover, autobiographical, reflecting a rather unusual life for a young lady in those days. While one could argue a literary precedent in Angelo Poliziano's May songs,[9] Jacopo Sannazaro's pastoral settings of his *Arcadia*,[10] and Torquato Tasso's play *Aminta*, it must be admitted that only Francesca's are realistic personal experiences. Francesca makes clear that a set of sonnets of her *Rime* are autobiographical, for she groups them together

---

[7] See Picot 121–22. Giovanni Turini's pension, received in 1549, amounted to 600 "*livres tournois*" (pounds coined in Tour).

[8] Most likely at the convent school of Santa Caterina, in Pesaro, which she attended for a short time.

[9] The humanist Poliziano (1454–1494) wrote poetry in Latin, Greek and Italian.

[10] The manuscript was completed in 1489, but the work was published in 1504.

under the subtitle "Principio dello stato dell'autore" [Beginning of the author's life]. The subtitle appears first at p. 80 (erroneously inserted by the printer and accompanied only by poem **1** of our edition) and then again at page 117, followed by the same poem **1** (but containing some variants), followed by the rest of the sonnet sequence. The masculine form *autore* is corrected to the feminine *autrice* (p. 117).

In moments of inner reflection, Turini Bufalini finds an intimate way of communicating with her room (**8**) and her bed (**9**). Although derived from a sonnet by Petrarch (*Rime, CCXXXIV*), her two poems achieve a personal tone in confessing her grief and youthful desperation for her lot. She was an orphan and probably had a modest dowry, which was still argued about at the death of her husband years later. The normal way out would have been to take the veil, and who knows whether this path in life was contemplated for her. Only late in life, in a moment of utter desperation, does Francesca state that the veil would have been a better choice (**111**).

It is curious to note that in describing her life at Gattara, she never mentions her cousins,[11] nor does she mention the frequent visitors from the Court of Urbino, or her own visits to Borgo Sansepolcro, where her brothers still lived in their paternal house.[12]

In 1574, at the age of almost twenty-one, Francesca was elated — she was asked in marriage by Giulio Bufalini, Count of San Giustino. Bufalini, a military man, had distinguished himself in Hungary and at Paliano[13] at the service of Pope Paul III. He lost his position for an unknown reason, but obtained new and greater favors from Pope Pius IV, including his title of

---

[11]Her uncle, Pietro Carpegna (1514–1586), had seven children from his first wife, Laura Monaldeschi della Cervara d'Orvieto (1531–1561). Francesco, their first-born, died in infancy. Tommaso (1560–1610), the second son, thus succeeded his father as count. Tommaso was born in Gattara. His mother died in 1661, during childbirth, along with her last baby girl. Tommaso's five sisters (all of whom married) preceded him and were close to Francesca's age. Pietro's four sons from his second wife, Francesca Bentivoglio di Gubbio (1535–1591), were born before Francesca married in 1574. See Carpegna Falconieri 129 and XXXII–XXXVII for Tommaso's life.

[12]Tradition has it that the house and tower on Via Chiasserini no. 47, at the corner of Via XX Settembre, in Borgo Sansepolcro, was the Turini building.

[13]A town in Lazio, about halfway between Rome and Frosinone, one of the most important feudal possessions of the Colonna family. In 1540, Ascanio Colonna refused to pay the new tax imposed on salt, so Paul III (pope from 1534–1549) sent his army against him. Paliano was the last of the Colonna towns to surrender in May 1541. See Caravale and Caracciolo 252–53.

count.[14] In 1573, he served Guidobaldo II of Urbino during the uprising of Pesaro. Count Carpegna and the Turini brothers, most likely encouraged by the Court of Urbino, gladly accepted Bufalini's offer, for he was powerful in Città di Castello (Umbria), where he was building a townhouse (begun 1572 but completed only in 1767) in the city center. Bufalini also possessed a castle in nearby San Giustino as well as a family palace in Rome,[15] useful for his long stays in the eternal city. He came to Gattara and Francesca was impressed by his manly bearing, his valor, intellect and his courteous manners (**14**). This marriage would restore Francesca's place in society, which she had lost with her father's death.

Giulio Bufalini, born in 1504 according to Mercati, was seventy years old when he married Francesca in 1574. He was a second-time widower, who had had ten children from his two former wives.[16] Only his daughters were still alive, in addition to his illegitimate, though legally recognized, son from an earlier relationship. He was obviously remarrying in order to produce a legitimate heir. Francesca did not seem to mind the great age difference of forty-nine years. She gladly took leave from her mountains, forests and shepherdesses (**15** and **16**), eager to take up her new life. She describes how she was escorted to her husband's home during a cold season that turned into spring for her sake (**17**).[17] She was greatly impressed by the Bufalini castle at San Giustino,[18] not only with its imposing building, consisting of courtyards, loggias, and a tower (all of it surrounded by a moat and gar-

---

[14]Pius IV (pope from 1559–1565) arranged the marriage of his niece, Dorotea Ferreri (whose mother was sister to Cardinal Carlo Borromeo, later declared a saint) to Ottavio, son of Giulio and his first wife, Giovanna del Monte Santa Maria. Unfortunately, Ottavio, born in 1542, died in 1569 while fighting in France, without leaving an heir. See Milani and Bà 38.

[15]It was later sold by his son Giulio (called II, to distinguish him from his father). What still can be admired in Rome is the Bufalini Chapel in the Church of Santa Maria Aracoeli, with fresco paintings by Pinturicchio (Bernardino di Betto), commissioned around 1485 by Nicolò Bufalini (great-grandfather to Giulio I) from Città di Castello, to glorify St. Bernardino, who had reconciled his family with their enemies, the Baglioni family (see *DBI* 14 (1972): 802–03 and Scarpellini and Silvestrelli 57–69).

[16]Four sons and five daughters from his first wife, Giovanna del Monte Santa Maria, and one daughter from his second wife, Elisabetta di Montevecchio, who died in childbirth in early 1574.

[17]The exact date is not known, but Francesca wrote a letter, dated Nov. 30, 1574, to her husband, lamenting his absence (see Milani and Bà 22). So the marriage must have taken place earlier that year, most likely in early spring.

[18]The Bufalini castle at San Giustino is still well-preserved. It belonged to the Bufalini family until the late twentieth century. In 1990 it became state property, administered by the *Soprintendenza per i beni ambientali, architettonici, artistici e storici dell'Umbria* [Man-

den), but also with its spacious rooms, finely decorated with fresco paintings[19] and statues (18). She found happiness with her husband in a "saintly love," as she states in poem 18. This marital tranquillity was interrupted by his sudden leave (20) for Rome where he had military duties. Francesca was desolate and wrote a number of poems lamenting his absence (21–42), in which she calls him her "spouse," "sun," "lord," and "beloved." She accuses him of cruelty for staying away so long, dreams of him and longs for him. The seasons change, but still he has not returned. She seeks solace in nature, but does not find it, though she produces sonnets populated with birds, flowers, trees, brooks and caves. In poem 30, she refers to the Bufalini castle under its proper name "San Giustino," which reflects her realistic autobiographical trend.

Francesca's grief was immense when she lost her first child prematurely (39). With this poem, the subject of miscarriage is treated for the first time by an Italian woman poet. Francesca describes how she almost died from the subsequent fever (40) and implores her husband to return home (41–42). Her joy therefore is great at his arrival, and her health is restored, along with her happiness, as expressed in poems 43–48.

In 1576, Turini Bufalini had a new theme to write about — her joy at the birth of her first-born son, Giulio. In sonnet 49, she rejoices for finally having given her husband his longed-for heir, while in poem 50, she pours out her maternal delights in kissing and embracing her baby. She returns to this theme in 1582 when her second son, Ottavio, is born (51). These compositions are the first of their kind in Italian literature. We will notice that no poem appears for the birth of her daughter, Camilla, born in 1579, at least not among those published. One might surmise the usual story — another unwanted girl among too many in the Bufalini family.

Life was not easy for Francesca. Her husband was frequently away for long periods of time, placing the management of his financially-troubled estate on her shoulders. Her five adult stepdaughters, hostile to her from the very beginning of the marriage, kept asking for money, as did Giulio Bufalini from Rome, but Francesca had none to give. There were continuous court litigations, with single individuals as well as with the communal administra-

---

agement for the preservation of natural, architectonic, artistic and historical monuments of Umbria].
[19]Done by Cristofano Gherardi (1508–1556) between 1538 and 1554, with long interruptions when he was away working elsewhere (see *DBI* 53 (1999): 544–48).

tion of Città di Castello, regarding some properties that did not securely belong to the Bufalini family, and Francesca had to deal with all of these affairs. She was also required to oversee the management of the family farms, both fields and livestock. In 1580, she even had to prepare an armed defense of the castle at San Giustino, when General Vincenzo Vitelli, instigated by his wife Faustina, surrounded the castle with 200 men, after a dispute over bricks ordered from a nearby furnace. Fortunately peace was restored by the governor of Città di Castello before any damage could be done.

A new misfortune struck when Count Bufalini died in Rome on February 5, 1583. On February 14, his body was brought back to Città di Castello (as he had requested), to be entombed in the Bufalini Chapel of the Convent Church of Sant'Agostino, on the 15th. He left a testament in which he appointed Francesca as the sole executor and administrator of all his properties, as well as guardian of his young children, and he indicated specific dowries for his daughters (Francesca's was to be returned to her). His first-born son, Giulio, was to have the absolute right to the Bufalini castle at San Giustino, while the other children, Ottavio and all the daughters, would have only the right to live there, since no division of property was granted. On the one hand, this established Francesca as head of the Bufalini family; on the other hand, it caused a lot of resentment against her, making her life more difficult.

At age thirty, Francesca adopted the black dress and veil of a widow, never to take them off again. She was left with three children of her own — the oldest, Giulio, not yet seven, the youngest, Ottavio, not yet one year old. She could not console herself and mourned her loss in a series of poems she defined as written for the death of her husband (**52–75**, included in her *Rime spirituali*). In these she accuses death of having struck her with another grief, while disdaining her own life — a life void of all joy (**52–58**). She implores God to take pity on her fatherless children, exposed to the greed of others (**59**). The children become an integral part of these sonnets in which she often questions whether there is any hope for them (**60–61**). Or she visits her garden and forest where she finds no consolation, for it seems to her that nature laments with her, while her tears flow abundantly (**62–63**). She finds no rest at night, tormented by memories of past happiness, or dreaming of her husband, so that she cries out for sleep and oblivion (**64–66**). Sonnet **67** is entirely addressed to the poet herself. She is looking in a mirror and sees her horrible black veil, her neglected hair, with the first white streaks among her blond tresses, and she rails against fortune which has brought her only torment. Once dedicated to music, song and poetry, now she is only capable of doleful lament (**68**). Just like the turtledove who cannot console herself, she too will continue to mourn her companion's death, without ever accepting a second love (**70**). Poems **71–74** indicate her desire to find peace in God by fleeing earthly things, which, however, she never completely managed to do. The last poem in this series, a madrigal (**75**), reveals Turini Bufalini's desire to be remembered, not for a great poetic style, but for her great sorrow — a sorrow that permits her to compete with Vittoria Colonna.

In spite of all the difficulties Turini Bufalini faced, she did not give up. She repeatedly traveled to Rome in search of protection which she succeeded in obtaining, and which helped her secure the Bufalini properties so that her children could be provided for in a dignified way. She stayed in Rome for long periods of time, where she was already known as a poet. (Her husband, proud of his wife's poetic talents, had shown her poems to his Roman friends and protectors.)[20] In 1595, while in Rome, and encouraged by her friends, Francesca published her first work, *Rime spirituali sopra i Misteri del Santissimo Rosario* [Spiritual Verses on the Mysteries of the Holy Rosary], dedicated to Pope Clement VIII. However, to the spiritual verses of the title she added, at the end of the book, twenty-four poems under the heading "In morte de l'illustrissimo signor Giulio Bufalini suo consorte" [For the death of the noble gentleman Giulio Bufalini her spouse], that is to say, poems **52–75** of our edition, discussed above.

After this publication, Francesca continued to write poetry, but published a new collection of poems only in 1627–28, under the generic title of *Rime* [Verses], which contains most of her autobiographical poems, including new compositions dealing with her husband's death and her sorrow, poems **76–101**, in which the tone gradually becomes more subdued. In these sonnets she, lamenting her cruel destiny, at first yearns for death (**76–77**), then implores pity from God not to abandon her in her desperation (**78**). She subsequently sees her husband in her dreams and is consoled by him (**79–80**). She even recalls his generous testament in poem **81**. Yet his splendid castle, with its surrounding garden, which she once described with admiration, seems empty to her now that he is gone (**82**). She recalls Città di Castello (under the Latin name of Tifernum), where she lived with him happily, only to see her heart enclosed in his tomb (**83**). Rather original is the sonnet in

---

[20]In his book, *Il ballarino* (Venezia, 1581), the dancing master, Fabrizio Caroso, active in Rome, dedicated a cascarda dance to her, titled "Meraviglie d'amore." The step description and music is preceded by a sonnet where he states that he has never seen Francesca, but has heard about her (137–38v written in by hand, since there is no pagination).

which she speaks directly to him complaining that he does not respond, until we realize only at the end of the poem that she is addressing his portrait (**85**). She communicates her grief to nature — to the little bird (**84**), to the water of the brook (**86**). While she sees others — the farmer, the fisherman — find rest at the end of a day's work, she finds no peace at all (**87**). Her bosom has grown cold with grief, similar to the mountains covered with snow in winter (**88**).

Perceiving her new situation as hopeless, Francesca repeatedly recalls with nostalgia the mountains and valleys where she spent her youth, as in poems **89–92**; the latter seems to describe an actual visit to Gattara, her uncle's castle where she grew up. Similarly, in poem **93**, while visiting her paternal house in Borgo Sansepolcro where her brothers were still living, she recalls, as she looks at the room where she was born, the glorious past of her father, a glory that disappeared with him. She continues to lament within a green setting of trees, flowers and grass, in poems **94**, **95**, and **97**, while in poem **96** she prays to be able to forget her husband so that she might turn solely to God. In poem **98** she states that her only consolation is writing poetry.

Francesca had decided to enlarge the burial space in the Bufalini Chapel in the Church of Sant'Agostino, in order to allow the entire Bufalini family to find a resting place there. For the work to be done, it was necessary to open her husband's tomb. Francesca was present and could not resist looking at his remains. The results of this viewing are two sonnets, without macabre descriptions, poems **99** and **100**, which consist of a series of rhetorical questions; in a third (**101**), she describes to him that she has had the family tomb enlarged.

Francesca found great consolation in her children, whom she dearly loved. Her poems express her readiness to fight for them and suffer for them (**102**). As Giulio grows older she sees in him a son with whom she can face the future, for together they would be stronger (**103**). In 1592, she writes a sonnet (**104**) for Ottavio's tenth birthday, and, full of motherly love as well as pride, urges him to keep up the valor of his family. But soon she must implore protection for him, from his guardian angel (**105**), from St. George (**106**) and from the Virgin Mary (**107**), because he is leaving for war at a very tender age. She anxiously awaits his return (**108**) and, upon his arrival, embraces him so emotionally that she doesn't know whether she is dead or alive (**109**).

Francesca's troubles, however, were not over and furthermore kept increasing. Her sons did not get along. Giulio was jealous of his younger brother, and accused his mother of preferring Ottavio. Ottavio, on the other hand, did not accept the fact that Giulio had been declared the legal sole heir by their father. Moreover, as they got older, they claimed that she, as administrator, kept them without money. They quarreled with each other, but together rebelled against her and in 1614 demanded that she yield to them the management of all their properties. Francesca, who had tried everything to bring about peace in the family (including taking them to court), could no longer withstand the emotional strain. She documents her new desperation in several poems. She first turns to her husband (in **110**), telling him that she cannot finish, as she had hoped, the buildings he had started, for her own children have turned against her. Because of her sons' quarrels, she now wishes she had chosen a convent, rather than marriage (**111**). She contemplates seeking refuge with her brother (**112**), and comes to the conclusion that she must go far away from her sons (**113**).[21]

In 1614, although no longer young, Francesca left Città di Castello for Rome in search of independence from her sons. There she became a lady-in-waiting to Lucrezia Tomacelli Colonna, wife of Constable Filippo Colonna, Duke of Paliano since 1611, and assumed the role of tutor to their two daughters, Anna and Vittoria.

In the meantime, her sons continued to quarrel. Ottavio, with a group of armed men, occupied the San Giustino castle while Giulio was away. Giulio retaliated by having Ottavio arrested and imprisoned. Francesca could only thank the Mother of God when he was liberated (**114**). Fortunately, the two brothers made peace in 1617, which Francesca took almost as a miracle (**115**). The occasion was Ottavio's marriage to Girolama Piscini.[22] A period of relative tranquillity followed. Francesca was happy in the Colonna household, where she came in contact with the Roman society, but was also able to make frequent trips to Città di Castello.

In 1622, however, her stay with the Colonnas came to an end with the death of Lucrezia Tomacelli,[23] whose illness and death Francesca laments in

---

[21]But she enjoyed an excellent relationship with her daughter, Camilla, who married Fabio, son of the Marquis Carlo del Monte Santa Maria.

[22]They will have a son, Giovanni Battista. See note 28.

[23]She died on Aug. 22, and was buried in the family tomb at Paliano. In 1625 her husband honored her with a monument erected in Rome in the Church of San Giovanni in Laterano (see P. Colonna and also Paschini.) The monument, work of Teodoro della Porta (1567–1638) and Giacomo Laurenziani (also spelled Lorenziani, who died in 1650), is located in the Colonna Chapel (formerly called Cappella del Coro), which is not open to the public. On the former, see *DBI* 37 (1989): 209–10; on the latter, see *Allgemeines Lexikon der*

a series of poems addressed to the Colonna family members.[24] She returned home, but a new tragedy awaited her. On August 10, 1623, Ottavio attended the festivities honoring San Lorenzo [St. Laurence], the patron saint of the nearby town of Cospaia, an independent little commune known as a nest of smugglers. During a dance, a quarrel broke out between two men over a woman. The men drew their arms, whereupon Ottavio intervened and separated them. Assuming that peace had been restored, he left with his servants, Pasquino and Livio, as most guests did, including Pietro, an armed guard. Out in the street, Pietro saw a man fall, struck by a harquebus[25] and, believing that his brother had been killed, drew his handgun. (Actually Livio, Ottavio's servant, had been shot.) In the next moment, Pietro was hit from behind in his right thigh. Turning, he saw that Pasquino (Ottavio's second servant), had fired the shot so he fired a shot in return, missed, and instead struck Ottavio in the back. Pietro panicked and fled toward the Tiber River, but Pasquino came running after him and repeatedly struck him with a knife. Found still alive, Pietro was taken to prison. He made a deposition of the events before dying of his wounds a few days later. Livio, Ottavio's servant, was killed immediately, while Ottavio died after having been taken to the Bufalini castle at San Giustino.[26]

Needless to say, Francesca was devastated and, given the bad blood that ran between her sons, a suspicion fell on Giulio, straining their relationship until the latter, sick and depressed, came to beg for her blessing. Ottavio's tragic end is documented in poems **116–119**, where she despairs that death has taken him instead of her. Especially moving is **118**, in which she states that she continues to see his cold, lifeless body. But when she sees the sick Giulio, she is terrified that death might take him as well (**120–121**).[27]

Poems **122–125** were written for her grandsons, for different occasions and at different times, but I have placed them together for their common subject. Poem **122** is full of tenderness for Ottavio's only son, Giovanni Battista, who had lost his mother as a baby, so that after the death of his father

---

Bildenden Künstler (Leipzig: E. A. Seemann, 1928) 22: 455.

[24]Not included in this edition, but in *Rime* (49–61). In the poem given on page 68 in *Rime*, Turini Bufalini states that she returned home "*poiché a l'alta mia Donna è chius' il giorno*" [because my noble Lady's day has come to a close].

[25]An early type of handgun.

[26]See Milani and Bà 55–56.

[27]Giulio died in 1642, one year after his mother.

he was left an orphan.[28] Francesca, as a grandmother, recalls how much she loved her son (who, as a baby, had also lost his father), and tries to find consolation in his child (whom she will raise with great dedication). She also includes three sonnets for two of Giulio's sons:[29] two for Giovanni — as a baby making her happy with his kisses, and for his first tournament (**123** and **125** respectively), and one for Nicolò — glorifying his achievements in his first tournament (**124**).

The remaining poems included in *Rime* do not deal with family matters. In them Francesca expresses a desire to find peace in God (**126**). She comments on how fast her youth has passed (**127**), or she seeks peace among nature and her Muses (**128–132**). She also uses the very common theme of old age, but in a rather personal way, by noticing her hair that has turned white (**133**), or by lamenting the loss of a tooth (**134**) — signs of an approaching death. Poems **135–139** are more literary and typical of the Baroque insistence on death. Poem **135** is a variation on a famous sonnet by Giambattista Marino, which describes man's cruel destiny from cradle to grave.[30] In poem **139**, she contemplates the head of a dead man, thinking that after death her own head is destined to become as horrible.

In the last two poems of our edition (**140** and **141**),[31] Francesca addresses the title hero of her unpublished narrative poem, *Florio,* who, she claims, sustained her throughout her many sorrows. She longs for night and the solitude and privacy of her bed ("a room of her own"), where she is free to immortalize Florio with her verses. So important is he to her that he, her creation, keeps her alive, as she confesses to him in a direct address. Such a direct com-

---

[28]Giovanni Battista, Ottavio's son, was born circa 1618 and died in 1670. He married Anna Maria Berioli. The Bufalini family continued from their descendants, up to the early twentieth century. In 1682, Anna Maria and her descendants received the title of marquises, not only for services rendered by her three sons to Francesco II d'Este, Duke of Modena, but also for their relationship — Alfonso IV had married, in 1655, Countess Laura Martinozzi, a niece of Cardinal Mazzarino (known in France as Jules Mazarin, for he was chief minister to the widow of Louis XIII and to her son Louis XIV. Mazzarino was the son of Ortensia Bufalini Mazzarino, daughter of a cousin to Giulio, Turini Bufalini's husband. See Mercati 7.

[29]Giulio had married Bianca Barbolani (1585–1625) and had ten children with her. Nicolò was born in 1611 and Giovanni in 1612.

[30]Marino's sonnet, in turn, was inspired by a part of the very long *canzone,* titled *Deus,* by Celio Magno (1536–1602), which had been published in 1597. The theme, however, goes back to the fifteenth century.

[31]Published for the first time by Corbucci in 1901 (53–54).

munication with one's character reflects an intimate relationship between the author and her literary creation and is rather modern in concept.

Hopes of returning to Rome to the Colonna household did not materialize, as the second wife of the duke did not want a poet under her roof. Francesca thus lived out the rest of her days in Città di Castello, in relative seclusion, until her death on April 25, 1641. She was buried next to her husband in the Church of Sant'Agostino, which no longer exists, having been destroyed by an earthquake in 1789 and later rebuilt in a different way.

Given her difficult and busy life, it is surprising that Turini Bufalini found time to write poetry and participate in cultural events of the two literary academies of Città di Castello, where she preferred to live in the palace built by her husband, staying there while he was away and especially after his death. She became a member of the local academy of the *Accinti,* and participated in some events of that of the *Agitati.* Later, she was also invited to become a member of the *Insensati* Academy of Perugia.

Among her literary friends stands out the poet and nobleman Capoleone Guelfucci (1541–1600), who encouraged Francesca to cultivate poetry and who read her early compositions in manuscript form. As a lawyer, he became her valued advisor in her complicated affairs, especially after her husband's death. She, in turn, encouraged him to write his religious heroic poem *Il Rosario della Madonna* [The Rosary of the Madonna], which he managed to complete in spite of an illness that tormented him for many years.[32] This friendship, at least on the part of Guelfucci, turned into love, probably a Platonic one, as is attested by the many poems he left in manuscript form, in which Francesca is mentioned by first and last names.[33] Francesca left no hints in her printed poems as to her feelings,[34] but in a manuscript sonnet, a reply to the playwright, Giovanni Battista Marzi,[35] who was a friend to both of them, she expresses her bewilderment at having lost her guide with Guelfucci's death.[36]

★★★★★

---

[32]The book was published posthumously by his sons in 1600, but his name appeared in it as Ghelfucci. It became popular and was praised, but was subsequently forgotten, for it is a work lacking poetic fantasy. See *DBI* 60 (2003): 568–70, and Ciferri 2: 148–53.

[33]These poems were erroneously attributed to Francesco Redi when published for the first time in 1837 by Ubaldo Pasqui, as was later pointed out by Gamurrini.

[34]She does declare that she refuses a "new ... second love" in order to stay faithful to her husband until her death (**70**, line 14).

[35]Giovanni Battista Marzi was well known in his native city, Città di Castello. He published seven plays between 1570 and 1617, some of which were reprinted several times.

[36]The poem was partially quoted by Torrioli 25, col. 1.

Francesca Turini Bufalini's first publication is a spiritual work, *Rime spiri-
tuali sopra i Misteri del Santissimo Rosario* [Spiritual Verses on the Mysteries of
the Holy Rosary], which was printed in 1595 in Rome. Her name appears
here in the old feminine form — Turina Bufalina. The book's religious sub-
ject reflects a trend started in the Renaissance and greatly cultivated in the
Baroque period.[37] Very appropriately, she dedicated it to Pope Clement VIII,
from whom she was seeking protection. In the two-and-a-half-pages-long
dedication (without pagination), written in a very elaborate, rather Baroque
prose with extremely long sentences, she not only compliments the Pope
and stresses the importance of religious poetry, but she also recalls her family's
service to the Church:

> [...] if Giovanni Turino, my father [...], and captain of famed memory in this
> world, died in the name of Christian soldiering, if Ottavio Bufalini, whose fa-
> ther's wife I was, died in France fighting against the heretics, if infinite others
> of this family and that of the Carpegna, from which I derive my maternal ori-
> gin, have served the Apostolic Seat, with the gown of profession and with
> arms,[38] and were highly compensated with prelacies and titles, it seemed to me
> a proper and necessary thing, of hereditary sequence, not to abandon that ves-
> tige, which I, as a woman, not being able to do with toil and blood, am forced
> to perpetuate as best as I can, with sincerity of affection and with devotion of
> ink. Not ceasing in the meantime from educating my two sons, one named
> Giulio, the other Ottavio, the former young the latter still a boy, both of not
> mediocre hope, and of very great consolation in my widowhood, so that they,
> just as the branches springing forth from a fruit-bearing plant, may bloom and
> produce fruit, at their time of marked virtue, in homage to the Holy Church.[39]

Fortunately, Francesca's poetry is simpler in style, not like her pompous
prose. The *Rime spirituali* is a very rare book today, and probably was printed

---

[37] Many works glorifying the Madonna were written throughout the centuries in Italy (see
Iannace). For the great number of spiritual works see Quondam, who lists 727 new titles
published between 1501–1600, 163 of which appeared in the decade 1590–1600 ("Note
sulla tradizione..." 211).

[38] As churchmen and as soldiers.

[39] The original Italian text is more ornate: *"[...] se Giovanni da Turino, padre a me [...], e
capitano al mondo di celebrata memoria, per lo nome morì della cristiana milizia, se Ot-
tavio Bufalini, del cui padre fui moglie, in Francia contro gli eretici, se altri infiniti di questa
e di casa Carpegna, ond'io traggo l'origine materna, hanno con la toga e con l'armi servito
alla Sede Apostolica, da quella compensati altamente di prelazie e di gradi, pareami debita*

in a limited number of copies. Fortunately, the complete text is now available in a modern edition, edited by Paolo Bà in 2005.[40] The book's spiritual portion, in which the author glorifies the main events of the New Testament, from the Annunciation to the death and Ascension of the Madonna, is divided into sections. The first one (pp. 1–50), titled "Primo Mistero del Santissimo Rosario detto Gaudioso" [The First Mystery of the most Sacred Rosary called Joyous], consists of 50 sonnets linked together in a continuous narrative, a technique used in all of the three mysteries. The opening verses introduce the subject:

> Awaken and rise, oh sluggish soul of mine,
> contemplate how the almighty Father,
> to liberate all of human kind,
> sends Gabriel, the angel, from Heaven on high.[41]

In describing the Annunciation, Turini Bufalini stresses the serenity and meekness of Mary who is not frightened by the angel but becomes timid and bashful at the praise he bestows on her, so that he must reassure her. The author then compares Mary to a rose and, in the manner of a Baroque painting, illuminates her by the rising sun:

> The sweet Virgin blushed at his words,
> her fair face turned the color of a rose
> that opens up as dawn appears.
>   And so, to hear her honest and dear
> notes, from the orient did the sun appear,
> the air turned milder and balm.[42]

---

e necessaria cosa, con ereditaria sequela di non abbandonar quella traccia, che io, come donna, non potendo con le fatiche e col sangue, sono tenuta a perpetuar come posso, con la sincerità dell'affetto e con la devozione dell'inchiostro. Non cessando fra tanto dalla educazione di due figli, l'un Giulio e Ottavio l'altro: quei giovine, e questi fanciullo, ambedue di non mediocre speranza, e solazzo estremo della viduità mia, acciochè, come rami sorgenti da fruttifera pianta, facciano e fiori e frutti al suo tempo di segnalata virtù in ossequio di Santa Chiesa" (n. p.: 2–3).

[40]My examples given here are, however, based on the 1595 edition.

[41]Svegliati e surgi, o pigra anima mia, / contempla come il Padre onnipotente, / per liberar tutta l'umana gente, / l'angelo Gabriel dal Cielo invia (1, lines 1–4).

[42]La dolcissima Virgo a quel parlare, / sparse il bel volto del color che suole / sparger ne l'alba in su l'aprir la rosa. / In tanto, per udir l'oneste e care / note, accostossi a l'oriente il sole, / l'aria fessi più dolce e rugiadosa (4, lines 9–14).

Turini Bufalini sees Mary as a human being, and she has her question the angel as to how the happy event will come about. Only after receiving an explanation does Mary meekly accept. The author then briefly mentions the encounter with Elisabeth, and describes the birth of Jesus, stressing the humble environment surrounding him, a baby born with a cry: "he whimpered nude in the straw and in the cold."[43] Yet at the same time she points out Mary's motherly joy which could be that of any mother:

Look at the mother and how her babe
she wraps in cloth and presses to her breast.
Look only at this aspect, forget all the rest.[44]

From here on Turini Bufalini follows the story of Christ until his entry into Jerusalem on Palm Sunday, with which the first mystery ends.

The second section (pp. 51–88), titled "Secondo Mistero del Santissimo Rosario detto Doloroso" [The Second Mystery of the most Sacred Rosario called Sorrowful], consists of 1 opening madrigal and 37 sonnets that complete the story of Christ and end with Mary crying under the cross. Her lament (or third section) is given under a separate heading (pp. 89–98): "Pianto della Madonna" [Lament of the Madonna], consisting of 20 octaves, in which her motherly grief is stressed. This is followed by the fourth section (pp. 99–139), titled "Terzo Mistero del Santissimo Rosario detto Glorioso" [The Third Mystery of the most Sacred Rosario called Glorious], consisting of 1 opening madrigal and 40 sonnets, which describe the events from Christ's resurrection to the death of the Madonna. The fifth section (pp. 140–148), titled "Ottave della Gloria del Paradiso" [Octaves on the Glory of Paradise], contains 25 octaves dedicated to the Ascension of the Madonna, whose importance is stressed in all the mysteries, to culminate in her coronation in Heaven.

While these spiritual poems are not always refined or original, the author's religious fervor is genuine in its simplicity and devotion, as she repeatedly, from the opening verses on, encourages her own soul to become involved, to repent and to love the Lord. Their literary value still needs to be studied against the background of the vast religious poetry published in the

---

[43] *Ei vagì nudo infra la paglia e 'l gelo* (13, line 14).
[44] *Mira la madre e come il pargoletto / ne 'panni 'nvolge e se lo stringe al petto: / questo sol mira, ogn'altro aspetto oblia* (15, lines 2–4).

second half of the sixteenth century. Following a Catholic literary tradition, Turini Bufalini inserted a glorification of Pope Clement VIII (to whom she dedicated her book and from whom she was seeking protection), as well as of his nephews, the Aldobrandini cardinals.

Of great importance for scholars of Italian literature are the 24 poems of the sixth and last section (pp. 149–172), that she added at the end of the book under the heading "In morte de l'illustrissimo Signor Giulio Bufalini suo consorte" [For the death of the noble gentleman Giulio Bufalini her spouse], consisting of 23 sonnets and 1 madrigal. These, stylistically, are of a better quality than the religious compositions, and have all been included in our edition of Turini Bufalini's autobiographical poems (52–75).

As the subtitle reveals, this last group of poems was written to lament the death of her husband. Published in 1595, they were not a new phenomenon. Vittoria Colonna, Veronica Gambara and Chiara Matraini preceded Turini Bufalini in composing poems mourning the death of their husbands or lover (in Matraini's case). Although we don't know what books Turini Bufalini read, she certainly must have been familiar with the first two writers, if not the last. Vittoria Colonna, whose *Rime* had gone through several editions in the sixteenth century, was her model. Francesca uses Colonna's metaphors by referring to her husband as her "sun" whose light shone upon her, while her own eyes, "dark lights," are obscured by tears. Yet Francesca's twenty-three sonnets are quite different from Colonna's compositions, in that the descriptions are more concrete: she visits her husband's tomb, she talks to its marble, she looks in the mirror at her horrible black dress and veil, she reveals her suffering to the nature which surrounds her, and she implores death with greater insistence. Her distinct innovation is the inclusion of her children in her grief.

The concluding poem of this last section (75) is remarkable, because in it Francesca measures herself against Vittoria Colonna. Perhaps that is why she set it apart from the solid series of sonnets by using a different metric form, that of a madrigal. She declares Vittoria Colonna meritorious of the spoils of poetic victory, because of a superior style, but she does not yield to her where grief is concerned. Francesca believes her grief to be greater than Colonna's and expresses her conviction that if her style were only equal to her piety and zeal, she, too, would brighten the sky with her Sun. Needless to say, this madrigal reveals Turini Bufalini's desire to be counted among the important Italian women poets. Yet, at the same time, she remains aware that her style was not as refined, for she lacked the proper literary education, as she will lament in poems published later.

Between 1595 and 1627, Turini Bufalini published two laudatory poems, one honoring Cardinal Cinzio (Cinthio) Aldobrandini in Segni's *Tempio* (1600), the other honoring Antonio Corvini, in Francucci's *Il trionfo celeste* (1616). Some of her sonnets of correspondence appeared in books by other poets, while seven of her personal poems were included in Guaccimani's anthology, *Raccolta di sonetti d'autori diversi* (1623). All seven of these poems will later be included in her *Rime,* though some with variants.

In 1627, Turini Bufalini published a collection of poems, *Rime,* in Città di Castello, consisting of 144 pages,[45] an edition so rare that it is not mentioned by any of the critics. I discovered a copy in the Vatican Library (call number: Barberini JJJ.II.9), a book that originally belonged to the Barberini family, as is evident from the binding bearing the coat of arms containing the three bees of the Barberini family and the column of the Colonna family. This edition seems to have been intended as a sample, for only a few persons, perhaps only for the Colonna family (whose coat of arms appears on the title-page), for it was reprinted in 1628 just as it was, with all the misprints and erroneous paginations, but with many additional poems added, to reach 313 pages. In other words, the 1627 edition contains the first part of the poems of the 1628 edition. At first glance, one could take the former to be a mutilated copy of the latter, but the dates of publication are clearly different and there are some variants in the dedications, both to Anna Colonna[46] (daughter of Filippo and Lucrezia Tomacelli Colonna), the first signed on January 1, 1627, the second on November 25, 1628. It is the 1628 edition which is always meant when referring to Turini Bufalini's *Rime,* unless otherwise indicated.

In the dedication to Anna Colonna, the author[47] declares that she had written her poems only to alleviate her sufferings, both those of her youth as well as those of her mature age. She also states that she had found a refuge from her own domestic troubles in the Colonna household.[48]

All the compositions of *Rime* are new. None of the poems of the *Rime spirituali* of 1595 are included, not even those on her husband's death. Only

---

[45]Page numbers 69–80 are mistakenly used twice but with different poems, and there is a jump from page 84 to page 95. Also missing are page numbers 111–12.

[46]The Vatican copy of Turini Bufalini's *Rime* of 1627 must have been Anna's, for she married a Barberini. See note 50.

[47]Her name appears as Turina Bufalini (not Bufalina as earlier).

[48]The Italian text reads as follows: "*Escono alla fine alla luce del mondo quelle mie rime che composte da me solamente per alleggerimento delle mie passioni, furono di non poco*

the seven sonnets from Guaccimani's anthology that had previously been
published appear again, but some with variants, as already stated. The first
group of sonnets, pp. 9–116, are almost all encomiastic poems dedicated to
Anna, to other members of the Colonna family, to their friends and members
of the Roman nobility.[49] The sheer number of these is overwhelming and
probably discouraged many a later reader from continuing to look for other
subjects. But on page 117 the best part of the collection starts — a set of au-
tobiographical poems, followed by those on various themes, such as the pass-
ing of time, death, or spiritual subjects. The book concludes with five
additional laudatory sonnets, two for her grandsons (**124–125**), one for a
baby girl born to the Barberini family,[50] and two for the King of France,
Louis XIII. The last one of these, rather Baroque in style, glorifies Louis' vic-
tory over the Huguenots at La Rochelle on October 28, 1628,[51] which
means that the *Rime* came off the press after that date, in November, as is
also evident from the dedication signed "November 25." The collection is
grouped as: sonnets up to page 265, madrigals, pages 266–299, a composition
of 26 *ottave* (stanzas of eight lines) on St. Mary Magdalene, pages 300–308,
and concludes with the five laudatory sonnets already mentioned, pages 309–
313. If we want to look for a structural frame, we can only say that the book
starts out and ends with encomiastic poems, but lacks any proportional dis-
tribution. This arrangement, of course, is no longer Petrarchan in structure,
but a free arrangement which was common in the Baroque period, although
already used by some poets of the sixteenth century, including Laura Batti-
ferri Ammannati, in her *Il primo libro delle opere toscane* [The first book of her

---

*refrigerio sì della travagliata mia gioventù, come della faticata età matura, finché nel colmo
delle domestiche mie sventure, per le continue discordie de' miei, quasi da procellosa tem-
pesta mi diede il Cielo sicuro porto nell'inclita casa di V[ostra] Ecc[ellenza], sotto l'ombra
della real colonna perpetuo sostegno della virtù e de' virtuosi tutti"* (3–4).

[49]It's a true gallery of princes and cardinals of the great families such as the Barberini,
Borghese, Ludovisi, Orsini, Montaldo, Aldobrandini, Capponi, Pio, etc., and includes three
popes: Urban VIII, still living, and his two predecessors: Paul V, and Gregory XV, as well
as several kings.

[50]The baby's name is not mentioned, but it must be the first daughter born to Anna Colonna,
who had married Taddeo Barberini, a nephew of Pope Urban VIII, on Oct. 24, 1627. Their
marriage ceremony was officiated by the Pope himself at the papal Castle of San Gandolfo.
See *DBI* 6 (1964): 180–82.

[51]A poem on the same subject by Claudio Achillini (1574–1642), *Sudate, o fochi, a preparar
metalli,* is now famous for its Baroque excesses (see Felici 64). It was, however, written
later, for the poet alludes to the 1629 French conquest of Casale as well.

Tuscan writings], which, however, is much briefer in length when compared to the more than three hundred pages of Turini Bufalini.

All the laudatory poems of *Rime* are preceded by the name of the person to whom they are dedicated, or include an explanation of the occasion for which they were written. The autobiographical poems are clearly identified as such by the already discussed subtitle "Principio dello stato dell'autrice" (p. 117), where the autobiographical compositions start. While frequently using the indication of *Nel medesimo soggetto* [On the same subject], Francesca never leaves us in the dark as to whom or to what she is referring. She tells us which of her children or grandchildren she is addressing, or what the subject of her poem is. These autobiographical poems are arranged in an approximate chronological order, with some incongruities; for example, the sonnets on the death of her son, Ottavio, precede those on his quarrels with his brother.

The fact that Turini Bufalini describes in detail her personal life is a novelty. Perhaps her lack of education saved her from writing like everyone else — imitating themes used by others. She was different and sought inspiration in the daily things that surrounded her. While the poems in *Rime* cover many years of her life, the way they appear in the printed text gives us no hint as to when they were composed. All her compositions describing her youth were rewritten for the 1627–28 edition, as she herself declares in the 1627 dedication to Anna Colonna: "they [the poems] have been revised and brought to the greatest perfection that my lowly talent was able to give them,"[52] a sentence not included in the 1628 edition. Therefore, in assigning her a place within the Italian literary tradition, what counts is the date of publication of her works and not the year of the events described in the poems.

Turini Bufalini, who lived from 1553–1641, felt the influence of various tendencies, as can be expected from her long life. As a poet she mainly wrote within the style of the Italian Renaissance still cultivated by some writers of her time. But she was also influenced by Tasso and was not immune to the Baroque style of the early seventeenth century, especially in her later poems. Her descriptions are filtered through a personal experience, an intimate contact with nature all her own, which enabled her to create vivid lyric impressions. In her poems we find forests, caves, brooks with torrid or limpid waters, trees of all kinds (oak, pine, laurel, beech and fir), valleys, gardens,

---

[52]"*[...] sono state da me rivedute e redott'alla maggior perfezione che s'è potuto dar loro dal mio umile ingegno*" (1627 edition of *Rime* 5).

bushes, colorful and fragrant flowers (roses, lilies, violets), birds, sunrises, springs, summers, and winters.

Turini Bufalini also creates for the reader a new kind of intimacy with inanimate objects, in addressing her room and bed, and in confessing her pain to them (in **8** and **9**), a device frequently used in the Romantic period, but not in the days when she wrote. Although inspired by Petrarch's sonnet, *O cameretta, che già fosti un porto* (CCXXXIV), she does not use any of his lines, nor does she paraphrase him in her two different poems. Moreover, her pain is of a different kind, that of an orphaned girl lamenting her cruel destiny, far from Petrarch's love-grief. Her keeping company with real shepherdesses, competing with them in running competitions, or just merry-making, was not a common pastime for a noble young lady of her period, nor is her roaming through fields and forests on horseback. But these descriptions reflect the great liberty she enjoyed in her uncle's castle, a liberty perhaps granted to her because she was an orphan. In her poems, she recorded her contact with nature, which was a real experience, not a poetic imagination as depicted in Jacopo Sannazaro's *Arcadia,* or as attributed to Erminia (while she lived among the shepherds), in Torquato Tasso's *Gerusalemme liberata* [*Jerusalem Delivered*], Canto VII, 1–174.

As Francesca's life changed, so did the themes of her poems. Marriage was at first all bliss, which then turned bitter, for her husband left her alone for long periods of time. The three sonnets (**49–51**) written for the births of her sons, in which she expresses her motherly joy, devotion and love for them, have no precedents in Italian literature. Later on, she will extend the same tenderness to her grandsons. The women poets of the sixteenth century, Vittoria Colonna, Isabella di Morra, Laura Terracina, Gaspara Stampa, and Laura Battiferri Ammannati had no children. Veronica Gambara did not write about her sons, while Chiara Matraini composed only a subdued and stylized sonnet on the death of her adult son (who had been hostile to her). In lamenting the death of her husband in the all new compositions of her *Rime,* Francesca, even when elaborating on the themes already used in poems of the 1595 edition of *Rime spirituali,* found a way to add new particulars. She is sorry that her youth did not prolong her husband's life (the only hint, but a positive one, at their age difference). At times, she communicates with him as if he were alive. She shares her grief with nature — with birds, caves, brooks, trees — stressing the seasons and their characteristics (the blooming spring and the icy winter). As a consequence, her poems are less gloomy than those of Vittoria Colonna, who preferred to use the imagery of lonely rocks in stormy seas. By including her young children in her grief, Francesca added another novel aspect to her poetry. Moreover, the poems on the death of her son, Ottavio, express an intimate, motherly sorrow, and are a far cry from the usual classical imitations by Turini Bufalini's male contemporaries in lamenting the loss of a son.

When writing on traditional themes, such as the inexorable passing of time, Turini Bufalini found a personal way of expressing herself. She looks at herself in a mirror, at her graying hair that used to be blond, or the loss of a tooth, all signs of old age, from which there is no escape. In her sonnet on human misery, written in imitation of the master of Baroque poetry, Giambattista Marino, we find an original detail — the description of the prenatal state of a human being where the womb is equated to a tomb. For Francesca, human misery starts before birth: the beginning of life is similar to the end of life — darkness in a tomb.

Other Baroque influences are evident in the sonnets on death, especially the one addressed to a dead man's head or skull, death's recurrent symbol, frequently depicted by painters and sculptors of the seventeenth century. Creating a more cheerful tone is the repeated use of the expression *caro mio ben* [my beloved], in reference to her husband, a phrase widely used in songs of the Baroque musical repertoire.

The spiritual poems of the *Rime* surpass, in style, those of the *Rime spirituali* of 1595. Together, however, these religious compositions attest to a profound religious belief, founded on the humble birth of Christ in a manger and on his and his mother's suffering reflected in all human pain and sorrow.

Composing poetry was for Turini Bufalini a true refuge from the ills of life, a mental therapy that brought her peace of mind. The fact that she had no classical education made her perhaps a more original poet, one who found inspiration in her own life and in her surroundings, and resulted in her choosing to write on subjects that were new in Italian literature. At times her style seems to lack refinement, but the simplicity of some of her verses, that read almost like prose, is deceptive, for the poems were purposely constructed as such. As far as I can determine, she favorably exceeds in originality other European women poets of her time, be they English, French, Spanish or German.

The *Saggio di sonetti sacri e profani,* that appeared in 1846, is a booklet consisting of a selection of Francesca's poems, published to celebrate the wedding (which took place in August 1846) of her descendant Marquis Filippo Bufalini to Countess Virginia Orlandi, formerly Princess Pallavicini, of Florence. Apparently, this booklet is available only in Città di Castello.

Among Turini Bufalini's unpublished works is a narrative poem, *Il Florio.*

The publisher of *Rime,* Santi Molinelli, in his "Letter to the Reader" which precedes the poems, refers to this piece as her major work, adding that it was almost completed. According to Corbucci, Turini Bufalini continued to work on the poem until 1640, when she sent the manuscript to her relative, Cardinal Ulderico di Carpegna,[53] asking for his opinion. His favorable reply is dated January 18, 1641. She died soon after, however, and no one thought of publishing the work or of attempting to locate it later. According to Giuseppe Milani, a manuscript missing its first pages, which he found among the Bufalini family papers, is a draft of this poem, and consists of 39 cantos. The main theme of the poem is the love of Florio for Biancofiore, a theme based on Giovanni Boccaccio's *Il Filocolo.* The poem still needs to be studied and compared with narrative poems written by other Italian women writers of the period, mainly Modesta Fonte's *Tredici canti del Floridoro* (1581) and Margherita Sarrocchi's *Scanderbeide* (1606, 1623).

Turini Bufalini also left some unpublished sonnets dedicated to famous Italian poets (i.e., Dante Alighieri, Francis Petrarch, Ludovico Ariosto, Torquato Tasso, Battista Guarini, Giambattista Marino, and Girolamo Fontanella), or addressed to minor writers (her contemporaries), and to her friends. These compositions, some of which were published in Corbucci's book (pp. 51–56), reveal her understanding of past and contemporary literary trends. For example, she called Marino the most harmonious poet ever, a greater charmer than Orpheus or the Sirens, capable of moving the wildest beast to pity with his lament.

The many letters, all unpublished, written to her husband, children and friends, are interesting documents concerning life in her time. Women, contrary to common belief, did not always lead a sheltered, inactive life. Turini Bufalini was more than an active wife. She not only had to hold together a family full of financial difficulties and discord, but she even suffered an armed assault in 1580. Yet in spite of all the adversities that befell her, Turini Bufalini conserved a sense of humor, for she cultivated burlesque poetry, mainly in the metric form of the madrigal, especially in old age, but which she never chose to publish. Igea Torrioli mentions this aspect of Francesca's oeuvre, which she illustrates in her article by giving three madrigals as an example. In one of these, Turini Bufalini pokes fun at herself — an old woman, good for nothing:

---

[53]Ulderico di Carpegna (1595–1679) was the son of Count Tommaso Carpegna, Francesca's cousin. He was made cardinal in 1633. See *DBI* 20 (1977): 594–96.

I lost my possessions,
my strength and my knowledge,
so that as a person
I'm no longer good at anything,
which causes me such great suffering
that's equal to dying.[54]

★★★★★

Turini Bufalini was known and respected for her literary endeavors by her contemporaries, but only within a limited circle, mainly among the intellectuals of Città di Castello, the nearby Perugia, and Rome, where she came in contact with the high society, religious and lay, gathered around the Colonna court. She became a member of the Città di Castello academy of the *Accinti,* as well as that of the *Insensati* of Perugia, which was highly regarded in those days. Her laudatory poems and sonnets of correspondence, which appeared in poetic collections or in books by others, are evidence that her work was appreciated and that she was in contact with poets such as Filippo Alberti, Antonio Bruni, Francesco Balducci, and Francesco della Valle.[55] The last three were friends of Marino and imitated his style.

In the eighteenth century, Giovanni Mario Crescimbeni briefly mentioned Turini Bufalini's publications in his *Comentarj,* as did Francesco Saverio Quadrio in his *Della storia e della ragione d'ogni poesia.* Luisa Bergalli, in her 1726 anthology, included only two religious poems by Turini Bufalini, the sonnet *Offerendo Maria l'Angel celeste,* and the madrigal *Rinchiudete le lagrime, serbate.* Bergalli took these from a seventeenth century collection of spiritual compositions, not from Francesca's published books, though she does mention the *Rime spirituali,* but not the *Rime,* thus allowing the autobiographical poems to go unnoticed.

In the nineteenth century, Turini Bufalini received a fleeting attention in England, when Isaac D'Israeli (1766–1848) mentioned her sonnet *"Ampie*

---

[54]*Ho perduto l'avere, / e le forze e 'l sapere, / sì, che la mia persona / in nessuna azion non è più buona, / che m'è di tal martire / che pareggia il morire* (Torrioli 35, col. 2).

[55]F. Alberti (1548–1612) served as chancellor in Perugia and was a member of the *Accademia degli Insensati.* A. Bruni (1593–1635) spent part of his life in Rome as did Francesco Balducci (1579–1642) and F. della Valle (c. 1600–c.1627). See *DBI* 1 (1960): 692; 14 (1972): 597–99; 5 (1963): 534–536; and 37 (1989): 748–50, respectively. Poems by the last three are included in Felici's *Poesia italiana del Seicento* 108–11; 106–07; and 164–65 respectively.

sale, ampie logge, ampio cortile" (see **18**) as a good example of descriptive poetry, in his *Curiosities of Literature.*[56] He quoted the poem and provided a translation — a better one was later done by J. Williams and published in *Notes and Queries,* in 1890,[57] as follows:

> Broad halls, broad courtyards, and broad galleries,
> and rooms with gracious pictures there I found,
> and noble marble sculpture stood around,
> of common chisel not the enterprise.
> A garden where perpetual April lies,
> and varied flowers and fruit and leaves abound.
> There is sweet shade and cooling fountain sound,
> and ways are there the same in beauty's guise;
> a castle that for safety doth possess
> a bridge and buttresses, and round it flows
> a moat of royal depth and ampleness.
> There dwell I with my lord; my spirit knows
> the bliss of holy love, and I can bless
> the day and hour that did my fate dispose.

In 1901, some of Turini Bufalini's poems were seriously analyzed by Corbucci, who praised their quality. Corbucci provided information on the Turini family, on Giulio Bufalini and on his wives and children. In reconstructing Francesca's life, he was, however, unable to trace her date of birth, estimated by him incorrectly as circa 1544. He believed the date given in the inscription, *"Fatto l'anno 1636 dell'età sua 85"* [Made in the year 1636 when aged 85 years], on a full-length portrait of Turini Bufalini, which once hung in the Bufalini Palace in Città di Castello, to be erroneous. We now know, however, that these dates are not more than two years off, because on July 23, 1636, Francesca had turned 83.[58] Corbucci's 61-page booklet is the text of a lecture he gave first in Città di Castello (on September 3, 1900) and then in Borgo Sansepolcro (on October 14, 1900). As such, it has an overtly oratorical intonation. Corbucci meant to glorify a local heroine (whose descendants were still living), and to reconstruct her life from her

---

[56](Local Descriptions) 5: 43–48.

[57]page 355.

[58]This inscription, as well as the lower one, identifying the sitter as "*Francesca Turina Contessa di Stiponigi Poetessa Moglie...,*" were obviously added later to the portrait and are incorrect. She never had the title of Countess of Stupinigi (Stiponigi). The painting, still in the Bufalini Palace, is reproduced on the frontispiece of our book.

poems, which he appreciated for their emotional sensibility and fine descriptions of nature. He did not, however, place her work within its historical period, nor did he compare her to other women writers, except for stating that Francesca did not need to envy Vittoria Colonna. At the end of his contribution, he included a selection from Turini Bufalini's unpublished poems: five sonnets on the poets Petrarch, Ariosto, Tasso, Guarini, and Marino, two sonnets on her narrative poem *Florio,* one madrigal, and some stanzas in which Venus describes her son Cupid and the havoc he creates. Corbucci also provided a list of fifty-seven poems, which includes those on the five poets listed above,[59] that he had seen in the archive of Giovanni Magherini-Graziani.[60] The sonnets on Florio, which Corbucci published, are important, for they attest to Turini Bufalini's "escape" into creative writing, the only consolation left to her.

In 1908, Hugues Vaganay, a librarian at the Université Catholique de Lyon, published, in *Romanische Forschungen,* the continuation of his comprehensive bibliographical list, "Sei secoli di corrispondenza poetica. Sonetti di proposta e risposta. Saggio di bibliografia," in which he gives the first lines of sonnets of correspondence exchanged between Italian poets in print. He includes Turini Bufalini's sonnets addressed to: 1. Filippo Alberti (published in his *Rime,* 1603, adding that they are not included in her *Rime,* 1628, which is correct); 2. Antonio Bruni (published in his *Le tre Grazie. Rime,* 1630); 3. Francesco Balducci (published in his *Rime,* 1645). Vaganay also includes Turini Bufalini's five sonnets of correspondence listed in Corbucci's booklet: two addressed to Tancredi di Borbone de' Marchesi di Sorbello and one each to Fra Tommaso, a capuchin monk from Gualdo, to Count Antonio Trissini and to Francesco della Valle (published in his *Rime,* 1622). Vaganay's bibliographical information is very useful for tracing Turini Bufalini's poems found in books by others. It also indicates that he was familiar with her *Rime,* as well as Corbucci's contribution.

---

[59] Actually only fifty-one are Turini Bufalini's, four of which had appeared in books by Marzi, Bruni, Balducci and F. della Valle; while six (#11, 19, 21, 49, 51 and 53) are sonnets addressed to her by other poets.

[60] Unfortunately this archive was dispersed. However, in the Civic Library of Città di Castello, the so-called "Quaderno Corbucci" [Corbucci's notebook] is still preserved, in which many of Francesca's poems had been copied, not all of them identical to those found in the Bufalini Archives. See Barni (81). Barni does not indicate which poems were included in Corbucci's book. On Magherini-Graziani (1852–1924), see Ciferri 3: 162–71.

In his 1930 article, "La lirica cinquecentesca," Benedetto Croce praised both Turini Bufalini's spiritual poems as well as those in which she evokes her life as a girl and as a wife. He appreciated their simplicity and candor, citing as an example the sonnet *Cara, fida, secreta cameretta* (8). But he considered Francesca strictly a poet of the sixteenth, not of the seventeenth century, because to him she seemed a typical, exemplary noble lady of the Renaissance, like Colonna or Gambara: well-versed, morally strong and with profound feelings, attributes he did not find typical of the Baroque period, as he later stated in "Donne letterate nel Seicento." As a consequence of his brief comments, the very same poem was included in Ponchiroli's *Lirici del Cinquecento* [Poets of the Sixteenth Century, 1958], and quoted in *Storia della Letteratura Italiana: il Cinquecento* [History of Italian Literature: The Sixteenth Century, 1966].

Unfortunately, past scholars, in writing about Turini Bufalini, ignored the fact that most of her poems appeared in 1627–1628 and had been rewritten for publication, when she was already familiar with the Baroque poets. These literary critics also failed to examine the contribution of Corbucci, already discussed, and that of Igea Torrioli, whose article appeared in 1940 in *L'alta valle del Tevere,* a hard-to-find periodical. In her article, Torrioli reconstructed the cultural ambience of Città di Castello, one of the Renaissance centers of Umbria, where painters as well as men of letters were active. She also provided information on the Turini and Bufalini families and illustrated the friendships which Francesca cultivated with other poets, including Guelfucci (Ghelfucci). In discussing the poems of *Rime,* Torrioli acutely observed that no one before Turini Bufalini had described childhood memories in such fine detail, or with such joyful tenderness a mother's love. Torrioli was also the first to point out that Francesca wrote comic poetry, as well.

In 1991, Alma Forlani and Marta Savini anthologized five sonnets by Turini Bufalini, thereby calling our attention to the work of this frequently-overlooked poet. The poem addressed to Marino is, however, erroneously cited as unpublished, since it had appeared in Corbucci's booklet. The editors refer to a doctoral thesis, "Francesca Turini Bufalini: una poetessa tosco-umbra del Cinque-Seicento," by Carmela Neri, completed in 1983 at the Univeristy of Perugia [Università di Perugia], which I was unable to see. In this thesis, Turini Bufalini's correct date of birth appears for the first time.

Recent studies on Turini Bufalini reflect the renewed interest in the local history of Città di Castello. Giuseppe Milani had access to the Bufalini archives and was able to add precise historical facts about the author's complex family matters, her children, stepchildren, and their descendants in his part of the book *I Bufalini di San Giustino*.... His comments on Francesca and her friendship with Guelfucci, as well as on her *Rime spirituali,* are mainly quotes from Torrioli which are not always properly acknowledged. Moreover, he gives the bibliographical reference of Torrioli's article, but not her name, in his note on p. 59 in regard to the cultural ambience of Città di Castello, and later refers back to it only twice. His notes lack precision in other cases, as well. Milani, however, located the first draft of *Florio* (which was considered lost) among the Bufalini family papers. Milani's coauthor, Paolo Bà, contributed the concluding chapter dealing with Turini Bufalini's style and versification, which he also examined in various articles published in *Pagine altotiberine.* Bà analyzed her themes, poetic techniques, and language, as reflected in her depiction of the Tiber Valley, in her evocation of youthful sufferings and enthusiasms, as well as in her emotional experience as a wife. He also gave us the first modern edition (2005) of Turini Bufalini's *Rime spirituali sopra i Misteri del Santissimo Rosario,* which he discussed in a subsequent article published in 2007.

Enrico Mercati conducted extensive research on the Bufalini family, from the early Middle Ages to the twentieth century and provided a genealogical tree. He is the only scholar to give 1504 as the year of birth for Giulio Bufalini, while others state that he died at age 77, which would make him two years younger. (Mercati, however, gave some obviously erroneous dates, such as February 25th for Giulio's death.[61] But Giulio died in Rome on February 5th and his funeral took place in Città di Castello on February 15th.) Laura Giangamboni examined Giulio Bufalini's last will. In 2001, Mercati and Giangamboni published the inventory and catalogue, *L'archivio e la biblioteca della famiglia Bufalini di San Giustino* [The Archives and Library of the Bufalini Family of San Giustino]. Among the many documents listed, there are quite a number regarding the frequent lawsuits Francesca faced, including those of her sons against her, or against each other. Also cited are letters Francesca wrote to her husband and to other family members, as well as a long list of letters addressed to her, which, hopefully, will be studied some day. Most disappointing, however, is the fact that the catalogue of the Bufalini library includes no books of poetry that may have been Francesca's and that may have, therefore, influenced her style. Of the twenty-two books

---

[61] And how could Giovanni Battista (see note 26), whose first wife died in 1645, marry Maria Berioli in 1638 if she was born in 1639? See Mercati and Giangamboni 266.

listed that were published before 1641 (the year Francesca died), only one is in verse, Guelfucci's *Il Rosario della Madonna,* but strangely a 1621 edition. So one can only wonder what happened to her private library. Was it deposited somewhere else or was it sold?

Turini Bufalini was included in *Dictionary of Literary Biography* volume 339: *Seventeenth-Century Italian Poets and Dramatists* (2008).[62] She deserves to be placed among the poets of the early seventeenth century, for her compositions were retouched before publication in 1627–1628, even if describing events of her youth. Her expressive poems are original for their precise confessional tone dealing with autobiographical events. At the same time, the poems offer a realistic, detailed life description of an Italian noble lady of the late sixteenth to early seventeenth century, one who had to withstand many financial and familial struggles, as well as repeated deaths in her family, during a period of political and religious strife, violence and armed assaults. A poetic calling gave Turini Bufalini the strength to endure. With regard to its influence, the work of Turini Bufalini may have had a direct effect on Petronilla Paolini Massimi (1663–1727), a later poet who lived in Rome, and who therefore may have known Turini Bufalini's *Rime.* Paolini Massimi described some aspects of her own life in a few poems that are, however, very different in style from her predecessor's. She also composed a prose autobiography only fragments of which are known.[63]

---

[62]See Costa-Zalessow, "Francesca Turini Bufalini."
[63]On Paolini Massimi, see Laurini and Costa-Zalessow's two articles.

The Bufalini castle at San Giustino. The deep moat is visible to the right, to the left, the arched portico (photo: A. Fontanelli).

One of the rooms in the Bufalini castle. Note the ornate cradle
(photo: A. Fontanelli).

The Bufalini Palace in Città di Castello. Now seat of the Circolo Tifernate.

BIBLIOGRAPHIES

WORKS BY FRANCESCA TURINI BUFALINI: BOOKS

Rime spirituali sopra i Misteri del Santissimo Rosario. Roma: Gigliotti, 1595.

Rime. Città di Castello: Molinelli, 1627.

Rime. Città di Castello: Molinelli, 1628, longer edition.

Saggio di sonetti sacri e profani all'illustre suo discendente Sig. Marchese Filippo Bufalini di Città di Castello, nel giorno 29 agosto 1846, in cui si sposa con la Signora Contessa Virginia Orlandi di Firenze, già Principessa Pallavicini. Città di Castello, n.p., 1846.

"*Rime spirituali sopra i Misteri del Santissimo Rosario.*" Ed. Paolo Bà. *Letteratura italiana antica* 6 (2005): 147–223.

POEMS IN ANTHOLOGIES, BOOKS BY OTHERS, OR REFERENCE WORKS IN CHRONOLOGICAL ORDER

Marzi, Giovanni Battista. *Ottavia Furiosa.* Firenze: Giusti, 1589. 7.

Segni, Giulio, ed. *Tempio. All'illustrissimo et reverendissimo signor Cinthio Aldobrandini, Cardinale S. Giorgio.* Bologna: Rossi, 1600. 291–92.

Alberti, Filippo. *Rime.* Venezia: G. B. Ciotti, 1603. 90.

Francucci, Scipione. *Il trionfo celeste, panegirico per la morte di Antonio Corvini.* Viterbo: Pietro et Agostino Discepoli, 1616. A4.

Della Valle, Francesco. *Rime.* Roma: 1622. Part 2: 179.

Guaccimani, Giacomo, ed. *Raccolta di sonetti d'autori diversi et eccellenti dell'età nostra.* Ravenna: Pietro de' Paoli e Giov. Battista Giovannelli, 1623. 48–51.

Bruni, Antonio. *Le tre grazie,* Roma: O. Ingrillan, 1630, p. 580.

Balducci, Francesco. *Le Rime,* Roma: F. Moneta, 1645. 441.

Bergalli, Luisa, ed. *Componimenti poetici delle più illustri rimatrici d'ogni secolo.* Venezia: Mora, 1726. Part 2: 77–78.

Corbucci, Vittorio. *Una poetessa umbra Francesca Turina Bufalini.* Città di Castello: Lapi, 1901. 51–56 (nine unpublished poems) and 57–61 (total list of all the fifty-seven manuscript poems from the Giovanni Magherini-Graziani archives).

Ponchiroli, Daniele, ed. *Lirici del Cinquecento.* Torino: UTET, 1958. 525.

Tuscano, Pasquale, ed. *Umbria (Letteratura delle regioni d'Italia, storia e testi,* ed. Pietro Gibellini e Gianna Oliva). Brescia: "La Scuola," 1988. 118–22.

Forlani, Alma, and Marta Savini, eds. *Scrittrici d'Italia.* Roma: Newton Compton, 1991. 77–80.

EDITORS'S BIGLIOGRAPHY: PRIMARY SOURCES

Bà, Paolo. "Due valli viste da una poetessa: Francesca Turina Bufalini già nota come

Francesca Turrini." *Pagine altotiberine* 12 (2000): 75–88.

———. "Pene ed entusiasmi giovanili di Francesca Turina Bufalini." *Pagine altotiberine* 13 (2001): 45–60.

———. "Francesca Turina sposa Giulio I. Bufalini." *Pagine altotiberine* 14 (2001): 113–30.

———. "Due poeti dell'Alta Valle del Tevere: Francesca Turina Bufalini e Nino Boriosi." *Pagine altotiberine* 22 (2004): 129–48.

———. "Il mondo di Francesca Turina Bufalini e le sue *Rime spirituali.*" *Letteratura Italiana Antica* 8 (2007): 485–94.

Bandello, Matteo. *Rime.* Ed. Massimo Danzi. Ferrara: Panini, 1989.

Barni, Daniele. "Alla ricerca dei manoscritti perduti di Vittorio Corbucci." *Pagine altotiberine* 21 (2003): 75–82.

Battiferri Ammannati (degli Ammannati), Laura. *Il primo libro delle opere toscane.* Ed. Enrico Maria Guidi. Urbino: Accademia Raffaello, 2000.

———. *I sette salmi penitenziali di David con alcuni sonetti spirituali.* Ed. Enrico Maria Guidi. Urbino: Accademia Raffaello, 2005.

Bembo, Pietro. *Prose della volgar lingua, Gli Asolani, Rime.* Ed. Carlo Dionisotti. Torino: TEA, 1989.

Caravale, Mario, and Alberto Caracciolo, eds. *Lo Stato Pontificio da Marino V a Pio IX* (Volume 14: *Storia d'Italia,* ed. Giuseppe Galasso). Torino: UTET, 1978.

Carpegna Falconieri, Tommaso, di, ed. *Terra e memoria: i libri di famiglia dei conti di Carpegna-Scavolino (secoli XVI–XVII).* (Studi Montefeltrani, Fonti 1). San Leo: Società di Studi Storici per il Montefeltro, 2000.

Catalogue des Actes de François Ier. (Collection des Ordonnances des Rois de France). Paris: Imprimerie Nationale, 1890. Vol. 4: 623, #13911; 1894. Vol. 6: 617, #22107 and 729, #22707; 1905. Vol. 8: 692, #32890.

Catalogue des Actes de Henry II. (Collection des Ordonnances des Rois de France). Paris: Imprimerie Nationale, 1979. Vol. 1: 306, #09.233; and Paris: CNRS Éditions, 1998–2001,. Vol. 5: 143, #8735; Vol. 6: 269, #11859.

Cecchi, Emilio, and Natalino Sapegno, eds. *Storia della letteratura italiana: Il Cinquecento.* Milano: Garzanti, 1966. 248.

Chieli, Francesca, ed. *Città di Castello.* Città di Castello: edimond, 2005. 84.

Ciferri, Elvio. *Tifernati illustri.* Città di Castello: l'altrapagina, 2000–2003.

Ciliberti, Galliano. *Il teatro degli Accademici Illuminati di Città di Castello.* Firenze: Olschki, 1995. 10–13.

Colonna, Prospero. *I Colonna dalle origini all'inizio del secolo XIX.* Roma: Istituto Nazionale Medico Farmacologico "Serono," 1927. 267–68.

Colonna, Vittoria. *Rime.* Ed. Alan Bullock. Roma-Bari: Laterza & Figli, 1982.

———. *Sonnets for Michelangelo: A Bilingual Edition.* Ed. and transl. Abigail Brundin. Chicago: U of Chicago P ("The Other Voice in Early Modern Europe"), 2005.

Corbucci, Vittorio. *Una poetessa umbra: Francesca Turina Bufalini.* Città di Castello: Lapi, 1901.

Costa-Zalessow, Natalia. *Scrittrici italiane dal XIII al XX secolo. Testi e critica.* Ravenna: Longo, 1982.

___. "Una prosa e due poesie dimenticate di Petronilla Paolini Massimi." *Forum Italicum* 34.2 (2000): 468–82.

___. "Fragments from an Autobiography: Petronilla Paolini Massimi's Struggle for Self-Assertion." *Italian Quarterly* 38.147–48 (Winter-Spring 2001): 27–35.

___. "Le Fantasie poetiche di Virginia Bazzani Cavazzoni." *Esperienze letterarie* 2 (2002):55–74.

___. "Francesca Turini Bufalini." *Dictionary of Literary Biography* (*DLB*) 339: *Seventeenth-Century Italian Poets and Dramatists.* Ed. Albert N. Mancini. Bruccoli Clark Layman, 2008. 271–76.

Cox, Virginia. *Women's Writing in Italy 1400–1650.* Baltimore: Johns Hopkins UP, 2008.

Crescimbeni, Giovanni Mario. *Dell'istoria della volgar poesia e Comentarj intorno alla medesima.* Venezia: Besegio, 1730. 4: 119.

Croce, Benedetto. "La lirica cinquecentesca," in his *Poesia popolare e poesia d'arte.* Napoli: Bibliopolis, 1991. 301–87.

___. "Donne letterate nel Seicento," in his *Nuovi saggi sulla letteratura italiana del Seicento.* Napoli: Bibliopolis, 2003. 165–82.

DBI = Dizionario biografico degli Italiani. Roma: Istituto della Enciclopedia Italiana, 1960–.

D'Israeli (Disraeli), Isaac. *Curiosities of Literature.* London: E. Moxon, 1834. 5: 43–48.

Du Bellay, Martin and Guillaume. *Mémoires.* Ed. V. L. Bourrilly and F. Vindry. Paris: Renouard, 1912. Vol. 3.

Felici, Lucio, ed. *Poesia italiana del Seicento.* Milano: Garzanti 1978.

Fonte (Pozzo), Moderata. *Tredici canti del Floridoro.* Venezia: Rampazetti, 1581; modern edition ed. Valeria Finucci. Modena: Mucchi, 1995.

___. *Floridoro: A Chivalric Romance.* Ed. Valeria Finucci. Chicago: U of Chicago P ("The Other Voice in Early Modern Europe"), 2006.

Franco, Veronica. *Poems and Selected Letters.* Ed. and transl. Ann R. Jones and Margaret F. Rosenthal. Chicago: U of Chicago P ("The Other Voice in Early Modern Europe"), 1998.

Gambara, Veronica. *Le Rime.* Ed. Allan Bullock. Firenze: Olschki & Perth: U of Western Australia, 1995.

Gamurrini, G. F. "Delle amorose poesie di Capoleone Guelfucci." *Bollettino della Regia Deputazione di Storia Patria per l'Umbria* 15 (1909): 321–33.

Ghelfucci (Guelfucci), Capoleone. *Il Rosario della Madonna.* Venezia: N. Polo, 1600.

Giachino, Luisella. "Tra celebrazione e mito. Il *Tempio* di Cinzio Aldobrandini." *Giornale storico della letteratura italiana* 118.178 (2001) 583: 404–19.

Giangamboni, Laura. "Il modello familiare e la trasformazione patrimoniale dei marchesi Bufalini nei secc. XV–XVI." *Pagine altotiberine* 2 (1997): 97–104.

___. "L'archivio storico dei marchesi Bufalini." *Pagine altotiberine* 4 (1998): 119–28.

____, and Enrico Mercati (see Mercati).

Iannace, Florinda M., ed. *Maria Vergine nella letteratura italiana.* Stony Brook, NY: Forum Italicum Publishing, 2000.

Laurini, Virginio Emanuele. *Petronilla Anna Maria Paolini poetessa di Magliano de'Marsi (1663–1726).* Roma: Lauri Novae, 1963.

Limperani, Gio. Paolo. *Istoria della Corsica.* Roma: Solomoni, 1779. Reprint: Sala Bolognese, Forni (in the series *Historiae urbium et regionum italiae rariores* 179 Nuova serie 95), 1990. 2: 383–98.

Magno, Celio. in *Lirici del Cinquecento.* Ed. Daniele Ponchirolli. Torino: UTET, 1958. 158–60.

Marinelli, Peter. "Narrative Poetry." *The Cambridge History of Italian Literature.* Ed. Peter Brand and Lino Pertile. Cambridge: Cambridge UP, 1996. 233–50.

Matraini, Chiara. *Rime e lettere.* Ed. Giovanna Rabitti (in *Scelta di curiosità letterarie inedite o rare dal secolo XIII al XIX,* dispensa CCLXXIX). Bologna: Commissione per i Testi di Lingua, 1989.

____. *Selected Poetry and Prose. A Bilingual Edition.* Ed. and transl. Elaine Maclachlan. Chicago: U of Chicago P ("The Other Voice in Early Modern Europe"), 2007.

Mercati, Enrico. "Cenni storici sulla famiglia Bufalini." *Bollettino della Deputazione di Storia Patria per l'Umbria* [Perugia] 94 (1997): 5–28.

____, and Laura Giangamboni. *L'archivio e la biblioteca della famiglia Bufalini di San Giustino.* (Soprintendenza Archivistica per l'Umbria.) Città di Castello: Petruzzi, 2001.

Milani, Giuseppe. "Il colonnello Giovanni Turini," *Pagine altotiberine* 2 (1997): 105–08.

____, and Paolo Bà. *I Bufalini di San Giustino: origine e ascesa di una casata — Francesca Turina Bufalini, poetessa 1553–1641: una donna che ha dato lustro a una famiglia.* San Giustino: Tipografia "Tiber," 1998.

Mirollo, James V. *Mannerism and Renaissance Poetry: Concept, Mode, Inner Design.* New Haven: Yale UP, 1984.

Morra, Isabella. *Rime.* Ed. Maria Antonietta Grignani. Roma: Salerno, 2000.

____. *Canzoniere. A Bilingual Edition.* Ed. and transl. Irene Musillo Mitchell. Lafayette, IN: Bordighera, 1998.

Oldcorn, Anthony. "Lyric Poetry." *The Cambridge History of Italian Literature.* Ed. Peter Brand and Lino Pertile. Cambridge: Cambridge UP, 1996. 251–76.

Paschini, Pio. *I Colonna (Le grandi famiglie romane, XI).* Roma: Istituto di Studi Romani Editore, 1955. 63–64.

Petrarca, Francesco. *Rime.* Ed. Ferdinando Neri, in *Rime, Trionfi e Poesie latine.* Milano: Ricciardi, 1951.

Picot, Émil. "Les Italiens en France au XVIᵉ Siècle." *Bulletin Italien* 1 (1901): 92–137.

Poliziano, Angelo. *Poesie volgari.* Ed. Francesco Bausi. Manziana (Roma): Vecchiarelli, 1997.

Quadrio, Francesco Saverio. *Della storia e della ragione d'ogni poesia.* Milano: Agnelli, 1739–1749. 2: 278.

Quondam, Amedeo. *Petrarchismo mediato.* Roma: Bulzoni, 1974.

___. "Note sulla tradizione della poesia spirituale e religiosa (parte prima)." *Paradigmi e tradizioni.* Ed. A. Quondam (Volume 16: "Studi e testi italiani," 2005): 127–211.

Ricotti, Ercole. *Storia delle compagnie di ventura in Italia.* Torino: Pomba, 1845. 4: 1–93.

Rosini, Corrado. *Città di Castello. Guida estetica della città dei dintorni e luoghi vicini.* Città di Castello: Nemo, 1961. 88–90 and 101–02.

Rozzo, Ugo. "Italian Literature on the Index." *Church, Censorship and Culture in Early Modern Italy.* Ed. Gigliola Fragnito. Cambridge: Cambridge UP, 2001. 194–222.

Sannazaro, Jacopo. *Opere volgari.* Ed. Alfredo Mauro. Bari: Laterza & Figli, 1961.

Sarrocchi, Margherita. *La Scanderbeide.* Roma: Facij, 1606, and revised longer version Roma: Fei, 1623.

___. *Scanderbeide.* Ed. and transl. Rinaldina Russell. Chicago: U of Chicago P ("The Other Voice in Early Modern Europe"), 2006.

Scarpellini, Pietro, and Maria Rita Silvestrelli. *Pintoricchio.* Milano: Motta, 2004. 57–69.

Stampa, Gaspara. *Rime.* Milano: Rizzoli, 1976.

___. *Selected Poems.* Ed. and transl. Laura A. Stortoni and Mary Prentice Lillie. New York: Italica P, 1994.

Tasso, Torquato. *Opere.* Ed. Bruno Maier. Milano: Rizzoli, 1963–1965. 5 vols. *Aminta* (1), *Rime* (1–2), *Gerusalemme liberata* (3).

Torrioli, Igea. "Francesca Turina Bufalini e la società colta tifernate nel sec. XVI." *L'alta valle del Tevere* 8 (special issue, 1940): 1–36.

Vaganay, Hugues. "Sei secoli di corrispondenza poetica. Sonetti di proposta e risposta. Saggio di bibliografia." *Romanische Forschungen* 21 (1908): 698–1112.

Williams, Jas. "Bufalini." *Notes and Queries* Ser. 7, 9.227 (3 May 1890): 355.

EDITORS'S BIBLIOGRAPHY: SECONDARY SOURCES

Beer, Marina. "Rappresentare se stesse nella letteratura italiana della prima metà del Cinquecento. Appunti sulle poetesse." *Mélanges de l'École Française de Rome: Italie et Mediterranee (Représentation et identité en Italie et en Europe (XVe–XIXe siecle)* 115 (2003): 89–106.

Benson, Pamela, and Victoria Kirkham, eds. *Strong Voices, Weak History. Early Women Writers & Canons in England, France, & Italy.* Ann Arbor: U of Michigan, 2005.

Bianchi, Stefano, ed. *Poetesse italiane del Cinquecento.* Milano: Mondadori (Oscar Classici), 2003.

Borsetto, Luciana. "Narciso ed Eco, figure e scrittura nella lirica femminile del Cinquecento." *Nel cerchio della luna.* Ed. Marina Zancan. Venezia: Marsilio, 1983.

171–233.

Chemello, Adriana. "Dall'encomio alla 'vita': alle origini della 'biografia letteraria' femminile." *Miscellanea di studi in onore di Giovanni da Pozzo.* Ed. Donatella Rasi. Roma: Antenore 2004. 191–242.

Coleschi, Lorenzo, and Franco Polcri. *La storia di Sansepolcro dalle origini al 1860.* Sansepolcro: Editrice C.L.E.A.T., 1966.

De Maio, Romeo. *Donna e Rinascimento.* Milano: Mondadori (Il Saggiatore), 1987.

Doglio, Maria Luisa, and Carlo Delcorno, eds. *Rime sacre dal Petrarca al Tasso.* Bologna: Il Mulino, 2005.

Erdmann, Axel. *My Gracious Silence: Women in the Mirror of 16th Century Printing in Western Europe.* Luzern: Gilhofer & Ranschburg, 1999.

Greer, Germaine, Susan Hastings, Jeslyn Medoff, and Melinda Sansone, eds. *Kissing the Rod: An Anthology of Seventeenth-Century Women's Verse.* New York: Noonday, 1989.

Jaffe, Irma B., with Gernando Colombardo. *Shining Eyes, Cruel Fortune: The Lives and Loves of Italian Renaissance Women Poets.* New York: Fordham UP, 2002.

Jelinek, Estelle C. ed. *Women's Autobiography.* Bloomington: Indiana UP, 1980.

Jiménez Faro, Luzmaria, ed. *Panorama antológico de poetisas españolas (siglos XV–XX).* Madrid: Ediciones Torremozas, 1987.

Kaminsky, Amy Katz, ed. *Water Lilies / Flores del agua: An Anthology of Spanish Women Writers from the Fifteenth through the Nineteenth Century.* Minneapolis: U of Minneapolis P, 1996.

Malato, Enrico, ed. *La fine del Cinquecento e il Seicento* (Volume V of *Storia della letteratura italiana*). Roma: Salerno, 1997.

Morandini, Giuliana, ed. *Sospiri e palpiti: scrittrici italiane del Seicento.* Genova: Marietti "1820," 2001.

Moulin, Jeanine, ed. *La poesie feminine du XIIe au XIXe siecle.* Vol 1. Paris: Éditions Seghers, 1966.

Navarro, Ana, ed. *Antología poética de escritoras de los siglos XVI y XVII.* Madrid: Editorial Castalia, 1989.

Panizza, Letizia, ed. *Women in Italian Renaissance Culture and Society.* Oxford: U of Oxford European Humanities Research Center, 2000.

____, and Sharon Wood, eds. *A History of Women Writing in Italy.* Cambridge: Cambridge UP, 2000.

Reich-Ranicki, Marcel, ed. *Frauen dichten anders: 181 Gedichte mit Interpretationen.* Frankfurt am Main/Leipzig: Insel. 1998.

Salzman, Paul. *Early Modern Women's Writing. An Anthology 1560–1700.* Oxford: Oxford UP, 2000.

Shapiro, Norman R. ed. and transl. *French Women Poets of Nine Centuries. A Bilingual Edition.* Baltimore: Johns Hopkins UP, 2008.

Stortoni, Laura Anna, ed. *Women Poets of the Italian Renaissance: Courtly Ladies & Courtesans.* New York: Italica P, 1997.

Van Dulmen, Andrea, ed. *Frauen: ein historisches Lesebuch.* München: C. H. Beck, 1991.

Volmer, Annett. *Die Ergreifung des Wortes: Autorschaft und Gattungsbewusstsein italienischer Autorinnen im 16. Jahrhundert.* Heidelberg: Universitätsverlag Winter, 2008.

Wynne-Davies, Marion, ed. *Women Poets of the Renaissance.* New York: Routledge, 1999.

NOTE ON THE ITALIAN TEXT

The text of the poems is based on Turini Bufalini's two published works: *Rime spirituali sopra i Misteri del Santissimo Rosario* (Roma: Gigliotti, 1595) and *Rime* (Città di Castello: Molinelli, 1628). All obvious printing errors were eliminated from the original text. The punctuation was updated. The unnecessary *h* was eliminated and the *j* changed to *i* or eliminated, as appropriate. The endings in *-ghe* (when used for *-che*) were changed to *-che*, as well as those in *-tione* to *-zione*. Uniformity was given to definite articles. The old future tense of verbs in *-are*, like *portarò*, was changed to *porterò*, where it did not interfere with the rhyme of the poem. Uniformity was given to some of the spelling.

The word *Sol* was capitalized when used by Turini Bufalini to refer to her husband, but not the word *signor* when used in the same way, as *Signor,* capitalized, stands for Lord (God) in her poems.

N. Costa-Zalessow

NOTE ON THE TRANSLATION

As a poetic invention, the sonnet is attributed to Giacomo da Lentini (c. 1215–c. 1250), who flourished within the Sicilian School of poets at the court of Frederick II during the first half of the thirteenth century. The poem consists of fourteen hendecasyllabic lines, the first eight grouped into two *quartine* or quatrains, to form the first two stanzas of four lines each, with a fixed rhyme scheme; the remaining six lines divided into two stanzas of three lines each, called *terzine* or tercets, with a more liberal rhyming pattern. Perfected and made popular by Francis Petrarch (1304–1374), the sonnet was much prized and imitated in its themes, metrics and rhyme pattern by poets throughout the Renaissance (and beyond), first in Italy and later in France, Spain and England.

Francesca Turini Bufalini, as a sonnet-writer of the seventeenth century, utilizes the metrics of the Petrarchan sonnet, its eleven-syllable line, as well as its strict end-rhyme pattern. At times, however, she diverges from the fixed pattern of the *quartine* (dictated during the Renaissance as ABBA+ABBA or ABAB+ABAB) and creates what may be regarded as an innovation in her choice to vary or alternate the end-rhyme pattern in the two *quartine* to ABAB+BABA (as in **2**, **10**, **17**, **24**, **27**, **37**, **50**, **59**, **109**, **111**, **118**, **131**; references set in bold type are poem numbers referring to this volume), to ABAB+BAAB (as in **135**) or to ABBA+BAAB (as in **68**, **108**). During the Renaissance, no deviation was acceptable within the rigid rhyme scheme of the quatrains — transgressions of this type being permitted only in poetry meant to be set to music, but not in standard literature. One does observe, however, that Petrarch's *Rime* contains an alternative end-rhyme pattern in the *quartine,* although used only four times.

In assessing a poetic achievement with regards to the sonnet, we may look to the derivation of the Italian word *sonetto* from the Provençal *sonet,* diminutive of *son,* which originally signified "melody" or a poem accompanied by music. In the sonnet as a metric form, although no longer set to music, the emphasis by and challenge to the poet throughout the centuries and in all languages has been to create a particular rhythm and sound that might render personal emotion into musical expression.

In rendering into English the rhymes of Francesca Turini Bufalini, I have attempted to reproduce some of the musicality of her poems. As Turini Bufalini chose to write, almost exclusively, in the sonnet form, I have, in these translations, tried to recreate her verses with as close an adherence to the beat of her hendecasyllabic line, or more often, with the use of the decasyllabic line preferred in English poetry. In a few instances, I deviated from the strict metrics of the line and diversified the meter, seeking to achieve a certain effect in English (for example, in sonnet **10**, where I hope in the English version to suggest the movement of a horse turning and leaping according to the whim of the rider).

In the majority of her sonnets, Turini Bufalini conforms to the Renaissance end-rhyme pattern of ABBA+ABBA or ABAB+ABAB within the *quartine*. At times, I was fortunate to find equivalent rhyming patterns for my English counterparts. Often, however, I fell short, and settled on an alternating rhyme scheme between the quatrains or on a separate set of parallel or alternating rhymes for each stanza. Where I found myself most challenged in recreating a full end-rhyme sound to correspond to Turini Bufalini's, I have sought a slant rhyme which I feel somewhat preserves the musical nature of the original.

Among Italian critics of literature, there is an old adage that goes: "*tra - duttore, traditore,*" which translates to "translator, traitor." The sonnet translator must make the inevitable decision of whether to drop a word in the source language in order to obtain a more musical effect in the translated version. In rendering these sonnets of Turini Bufalini, I have sacrificed an adjective or verb of the original if the loss did not detract from the content or effect that the Italian piece creates as a whole. In doing so, I have attempted to bring into greater relief in English the rhythmic quality of the poetic form. I have also, in a few instances, elected to add an adjective or noun, in an effort to recreate the musicality of the poem's internal or end-rhyme, and only if in keeping with the intent of the original. The rhyme and meter of the Italian sonnet are the heartbeat of the form. As a translator, I hoped to bring these qualities into the English counterpart, wherever possible, and to preserve the resonance of the original and the pleasure that rhyme and meter afford to the ear.

Francesca Turini Bufalini, writing in the shadow of her eminent predecessor and sonneteer, Vittoria Colonna, was most conscious of what she perceived in herself to be a lack of equal style. She chooses to address Colonna, not with a sonnet, but with a madrigal (**75**). In this poem, Turini Bufalini poses that Colonna will remain, to posterity, the greater for her art (*stile*), the sound of her learned and angelic words (*il suon di dotte, angeliche parole*), and her renowned rhyme (*rime alte e famose*). At the same time, however, Turini Bufalini would claim for herself an equal piousness of feeling, a greater weeping (*pianto*) and a deeper sorrow (*dolore*). I would also claim for her an intimacy and immediacy of voice.

It is my hope that these translations of Turini Bufalini's poems, which in the Italian display much beauty of tone and rhythm, and of heartfelt emotion, create for the English reader the very human and timeless sound both of sorrow and of joy.

Joan E. Borrelli

Nascita e giovinezza fino al matrimonio

1.

Note the repeated use of the harsh *p* sound in line 14 to indicate the hard life of the author as a child. It recalls Tasso's *il pietoso pastor pianse al suo pianto* (*Gerusalemme liberata*, VII, 16, line 8). Petrarch defined himself as *a pianger nato* (*Rime*, CXXX, 6), but his suffering was caused by love.

> Di dominio, di aver, d'opre, di onore
> era nel colmo il mio paterno nido,
> quando, misera, apersi in questo infido
> mondo gli occhi a le lagrime, al dolore,   4
>   ché tosto priva fui del genitore,
> onde poscia cangiai fortuna e lido
> con la mia madre, e de l'amato e fido
> albergo uscimmo, lagrimando, fuore.
>   Né qui fermò, ché la mia sorte ingrata   8
> nel maggior uopo ancor mi tolse lei,
> onde fui in tutto dei parenti orbata.   11
>   Nel libero Catai crebbi ed amata
> fui dal materno zio che i danni miei
> pianse pietoso, sol per pianger nata.   14

2.

The author complains that her studies were *deboli e lenti* [weak and slow], line 3. Note the rarely used alternative rhyme in the *quartine*: ABAB/BABA. (See "Translator's Note.")

> Mentre menava i giorni miei dolenti,
> ancor fanciulla, in queste parti e in quelle,
> furon gli studi miei deboli e lenti.
> L'ore traendo con le pastorelle,   4
>   godea di veder le pecorelle
> pascer l'erbette e bere ai rii correnti,
> premer il latte e trar da le mammelle,

From Childhood to Marriage

The poems in this section, **1–16**, are from *Rime* (117–32).

1.

    Of power, honored deeds, possessions, pride
did my belovèd father's house brim full,
when first, alas, my eyes opened, espied
tears and pain only, in this faithless world;   4
    for all too soon was I deprived of him,
to altered luck and to unknown shores tossed,
when with my mother, forth from that safe home,
weeping, we set out together, lost.   8
    Nor did it end, for by ungrateful fate,
in my worst state was she then from me cleft;
of father, mother was I thus bereft.   11
    In free Cathay[1] I lived, and loved was I,
raised by her manly kin, who scorn so great
with mercy mourned; I born only to cry.[2]   14

2.[3]

    While yet a girl, I'd spend sorrowful days
wandering into these parts, into those;
how weak and slow was I then with my studies.
With shepherdesses I would pass the hours;   4
    I loved to see the sheep, amid the flowers,
put out to drink at quickened brooks and graze;
and then the flock, led back to humble bowers,

---

[1]*Catai* in Italian, or Cathay in English, the fantastic land of China, as described in narrative poems, represents the castle of Gattara, home of her maternal uncle, Count Pietro Carpegna.
[2]Refers back to the beginning of the sentence: I born only to cry, lived in free Cathay.
[3]This sonnet recalls Tasso's description of Erminia among the shepherds in his *Gerusalemme liberata* (*Jerusalem Delivered,* Canto VII, 18, lines 5–8).

ricondotti a l'ovil gli umili armenti.   8
   Or fiscelle intessea fra l'ombre amene,
cantando, e poi l'empìa di gigli e rose,
di che tutte eran quelle rive piene.   11
   Or, al suon de la cetra, artifiziose
danze guidava a minuir mie pene,
che fur quinci men gravi e men dogliose.   14

3.

This sonnet continues the theme of the preceding one, for the author laments that the lack of proper studies left her crippled, and alludes to Vulcan, the Roman god of fire and metal-working — a smith (*fabbro*) who was lame. Therefore, she must work hard, and her fatigue is reflected in the words *fabbro, affatico, fabbricarmi* (lines 9–11) and continues with the rhyming words *sudo, schermo, scudo* (lines 10–12). Note that lines 5–6 derive from Bembo's *Dive [...] / use far a la morte illustri inganni* (Introductory sonnet, I, lines 5–6).

   Quand' era il tempo, ohimè, di spender gl'anni
nei bei studi di Palla e l'intelletto
fregiar di lumi, in chiuso ermo ricetto
solo a pianger appresi i propri danni.   4
   E di tesser invece illustri inganni
a Morte, fu per le mie mani eletto
il fuso e l'ago, ancor che 'l mio diletto
fosse ad eccelsa meta ergere i vanni.   8
   Or, mal esperto fabbro al fianco infermo,
con debil lena mi affatico e sudo
contro a l'oblìo di fabbricarmi schermo,   11
   ché, dove il frale aver riparo e scudo,
col dì fatal non può: stabile e fermo
rimanga il nome e non di gloria ignudo.   14

milk pressed from flowing udders, took my gaze.   8
    While singing, I'd weave baskets in the shade,
fill them with lilies, roses, in a sheaf,
buds which the riverbanks amply displayed.   11
    At times, with pluck of cithara[4] I'd lead
an artful round of dance to lessen grief,
which grew less grave, from which I found relief.   14

3.

    When the time came for me to take my flight
in Pallas'[5] sublime pursuits and to adorn
the intellect with light, instead, in hermetic respite,
I only learned to grieve my life, forlorn.[6]   4
    And when I would have loved with such delight
to weave against Death renowned contrabands
and lift my wings to much loftier height,
I found spindle and needle in my hands.   8
    Now, inexperienced smith with infirm gait,
with weakened breath, I toil and sweat my story,
to forge a sheath against oblivion,   11
    for if I work to shield my fragile gift,
it will not end with death; forever strong
may my name remain, and not bare of glory.   14

---

[4]Italian does not distinguish by name the ancient string instrument from the more recent zither.
[5]Pallas Athene, Greek goddess of wisdom.
[6]The poem probably alludes to a convent school to which she was sent.

4.

Lines 5–6, in which Echo answers the poet, may have been influenced by Poliziano's *a' sua lamenti Eco risponde* (*Stanze per la giostra*, 60, line 5), Sannazaro's *Eco mesta, rispondi a le parole* (*Arcadia*, XI, poem, line 14), or Tasso's *Eco, e tu che rispondi al mio lamento* (*Rime*, 309, line 5).

> Per trapassare i dì noiosi e gravi,
> in cara solitudine romita
> or l'anima con Dio tenni rapita,
> or con suoni accordai voci soavi,   4
> ed or mi rispondea da sassi cavi
> Eco, che in quelle grotte ha spirto e vita,
> che m'era via più dolce e più gradita
> che le canne di Cipro o d'Ibla i favi.   8
> E per quei boschi salutare il giorno
> udìa gli augelli e rimirava l'onde
> chiare irrigar quelle campagne intorno.   11
> Trassi talor su le fiorite sponde
> con le mie Muse un placido soggiorno,
> io di lor vaga ed esse a me seconde.   14

5.

Silvia, in Tasso's *Aminta*, adorned herself with flowers while gazing at her reflection in the waters of a lake (II, 2, lines 850–86).

> Ahi, quante volte, per temprar mia doglia,
> l'ore del dì menava entro al giardino,
> a l'ombra d'un abete o pur d'un pino,
> incidendo il mio duol ne la loro spoglia.   4
> Ed or, d'un antro ombroso in su la soglia,
> con questo e con quel garrulo augellino
> gareggiava, che udìa cantar vicino
> e sicuro scherzar tra foglia e foglia.   8
> Ed or, ne l'acque cristalline e belle,
> lavando il volto e 'l sen, prendea diletto,
> e poscia specchio mi facea di quelle.   11
> Or mi ornava di fior le chiome e 'l petto,
> e così di Fortuna le procelle
> temprai, rivolta a più tranquillo affetto.   14

4.

In lonely, dear, hermetic solitude,
to walk myself through hours most tedious,
at times I kept my soul enrapt with God,
at times I tuned with subtle sounds my voice,   4
    and from the rocky caves sometimes responded
Echo, who in grottoes makes her home,
and who more sweet, more welcome to me, sounded
than Cyprus'[7] flutes or Hybla's[8] honeycombs.   8
    And through those thronging woods, to greet the day,
I'd hear bird cry resound, and I would see
clear waves watering all the lands around.   11
    On those blossoming banks, a peace, profound,
I savored with my Muses, in this way;
I, longing for them, they favoring me.   14

5.

Oh, many, many times my pain to temper,
in gardens would my hours seem most brief,
within the shade of pine tree or of fir,
as in their barks I would engrave my grief.   4
    And with this or that garrulous little bird,
while sheltered by a cave in shady eaves,
I would compete, whom singing I had heard
as he hopped happily among the leaves.   8
    At times, with waters so crystalline-bright,
in washing face and bosom I'd delight,
and there would I see mirrored my reflection.   11
    Then I'd adorn with flowers my hair and breasts,
and in this way I found that Fortune's tempests
I tempered, turned to more tranquil affection.   14

---

[7]Island sacred to the goddess of love, Aphrodite (Venus).
[8]A mountain in Sicily, later called Megara, famous for its honey.

6.

This sonnet, glorifying the month of May, reminds us of Poliziano, but differs in that there is no allusion to love. It is just a merry song of shepherdesses, without secondary aims, which enchants the animals of the forest, as did the songs of Orpheus.

Per onorare il bel fiorito maggio
con quelle pastorelle pellegrine,
succinta in gonna, inghirlandata il crine,
pronta mi mossi in su l'aprir del raggio.   4
    E con soave stil, benché selvaggio
spiegavam le grandezze, alme e divine,
di sì bel giorno, onde le fere alpine
non prendean, per udirci, altro viaggio.   8
    E i cembali accordando ai nostri accenti
formavam sì soave melodia
che stavan tutti ai dolci canti intenti.   11
    Così temprai la doglia acerba e ria,
ché modi ha la virtù così potenti,
ch'ogni amaro pensier dal cor disvia.   14

7.

Molti tuguri io mi vedea d'intorno,
qual sovra un colle e qual sovra d'un monte,
a questi spesso io rivolgea la fronte
per trapassar con minor noia il giorno.   4
    E quante pastorelle in quel contorno
eran, venian per aggradirmi pronte,
ed a l'ombra d'un faggio, a un chiaro fonte,
spesso traea con lor dolce soggiorno.   8
    E al suon di pastorale cetra o piva,
gareggiando cantar note amorose,
sì che a sentirle avea sommo diletto.   11
    E le vincenti inghirlandai di rose
di mia man colte per maggior affetto,
così la vita mia mantenni viva.   14

6.

Astride with all the wandering shepherdesses,
to honor the bright blooms in month of May,
my skirt tucked up, flowers in my tresses,
I'd start out at the break of sun's first ray.   4
And in a lovely style, albeit artless,
would we intone the splendor, divine, gay,
of such a wondrous day, as mountain beasts
would rest their tracks to hear us, and not stray.   8
Attuning tambourines to our accent,
would we create a melody so fine,
that all stood still, on our sweet songs intent.   11
Thus did I mitigate my caustic pain,
for music with it potent influence
diverts the heart, so grief cannot remain.   14

7.

The many huts I saw around that place,
some on a hill, others upon a mountain,
so often to these would I turn my face
to spend my day with lessened tedium.   4
And shepherdesses many as there were
would come and congregate, ready to cheer me;
upon me pleasant stay would they confer
nearby clear springs within the shade of beech tree.   8
And with bagpipe or cithara[9] in play,
competing, melodies of love they'd sing
while I took great delight in listening.   11
The winners I would then with roses garland,
roses made dear, as chosen by my hand;
and so I kept my life alive this way.   14

---

[9]Ancient string instrument.

8.

Inspired by Petrarch's *O cameretta, che già fosti un porto* (*Rime*, CCXXXIV), but personal and feminine, a room of her own (a concept made famous in modern times by Virginia Woolf), where she found refuge and was at liberty to cry or engage in various activities.

Cara, fida, secreta cameretta,
in cui passai dolente i miei verd' anni,
e 'n cui la notte e 'l dì piansi i miei danni,
mentre in te mi vedea chiusa e soletta.   4
    Quanto, in ogni stagion, fosti diletta,
alternando a me stessa i fregi e i panni,
ed a vari pensier spiegando i vanni,
o suonando, o leggendo opera eletta.   8
    Or con trapunti il giorno iva passando,
or con le Muse al fonte d'Elicona,
ponendo in tutto ogni altra cura in bando,   11
    ché a questo ogni altro ben non paragona,
né dolcezza è maggior di quella, quando
con lor dolce si canta e si ragiona.   14

9.

This sonnet continues the influence of the same Petrarchan poem mentioned above, that is, his line 5, *O letticciuol, che requie eri e conforto*, but Turini Bufalini eliminates the diminutive *letticciuol*, rightly preferring the use of *letto*, where she could cry without being seen. Her use of *bagnar [...] lagrimando* and then to *rasciugar [...] coi sospir ardenti* (lines 7–8), is rather Baroque.

Letto, porto fedel dei miei lamenti,
in cui doleami di mia trista sorte,
e sicura al mio duolo apria le porte,
quand' erano del giorno i raggi spenti.   4
    Quanto fur dolorosi i miei tormenti!
Quante volte mi udisti chiamar Morte,
quante bagnarti lagrimando forte,
poi rasciugarti coi sospir ardenti.   8
    Ma pur giungendo il sonno in su l'albore,
temprasti la notturna mia fatica,
sparso d'oblio soave il mio dolore.   11

8.[10]

Dear, faithful, secret little room,
in which I spent, afflicted, my green years,
wherein I saw myself cloistered, alone,
and where, morning and night, I shed my tears;   4
    in every month were you belovèd thing
wherein I changed my ornaments and clothes,
and to my sundry thoughts spread out my wings,
while reading noble words, or with my Muse.   8
    At times, with needlework I'd spend my day,
or dwell with those who dwell at Helicon's[11] spring,
and so put every other care away,   11
    for nothing else can this great sweetness bring,
no other good compare, when one can stay
sweetly with them, to reason and to sing.   14

9.

Bed, of my laments a faithful port,
wherein I complained much of my sad plight,
so sheltered, to my pain the doors I sought,
opened as sun faded into night.   4
    How painful were my torments, infinite!
How many times you heard me call on Death,
how many times I drenched you, cried outright,
then, sighing, dried you with my ardent breath.   8
    But somehow sleep would come to me at dawn,
and you would temper my nocturnal fight
and on my pain shed soft oblivion.   11

---

[10]Although they derive from Petrarch, this poem and the next one, **9**, are remarkable for the confidential tone that the author assumes in addressing inanimate objects, such as her room and her bed, witnesses to her torments.
[11]Mountain in Greece, home of the Muses.

Ond' or, s'io penso a la tua piuma amica,
ritorna la tua pace entro al mio core,
riconoscendo la dolcezza antica.   14

10.

In order to appreciate the originality of this sonnet by Turini Bufalini, compare it to the poem, *Bella donna a cavallo,* by Girolamo Preti (1582–1626), who describes the horse and the lady who *pungea / con lo sprone il destrier, col guardo i cori* (Felici, p. 68–69, lines 13–14), but where there is no riding involved. Note the alternative rhyme in the *quartine*: ABAB/BABA.

Talor, per dare al mio dolor soccorso
e serenare il torbido pensiero,
a un agile destrier premeva il dorso,
che la mano obedìa presto e leggiero.   4
    E prendendo il più facile sentiero,
or di galoppo, or lo stendeva al corso,
che ben ch'egli sen gisse ardito e fiero,   8
resil, volendo, obediente al morso.
    Ed or a la sinistra, or a la destra
raddoppiar li faceva angusti giri,
come mi suggeriva arte maestra.   11
    Ed or, dovunque il fiumicel si aggiri,
saltando, o su per una rupe alpestra,
ché il periglio il piacer fa che non miri.   14

11.

Or Camilla, la Volsca, imitar volsi,
che nel correr le piante ebbe sì snelle,
ed al corso sfidai le pastorelle,
e del mio fatigar frutto raccolsi.   4
    Ché con le più veloci il passo sciolsi,
e vincente restai spesso di quelle,
tant' ebbi favorevoli le stelle,
e a tutte l'altre il plauso e 'l premio tolsi.   8
    Ond' or di ghirlandette il crin mi ornaro,
ed or d'un pastoral mirto nodoso,

And so, when of your feathers I now think,
into a friendly peace does my heart sink
to recognize again that sweetness gone.   14

10.

When I no more could troubled thoughts abide,
at times I'd find relief from my distress
upon the back of a fine steed to ride,
one fast and agile, prone to my finesse.   4
    And though he'd, bold and proud, opt his own pace,
I'd hit upon a course both quick and wide.
I'd pull the bit until he'd acquiesce,
and force him into galloping full stride.   8
    Now to the left, now to the right,
I'd take him through sharp turns,
beneath the guide of my masterly skill.   11
    Now where a brook ran out of sight,
we'd jump, and neither steep cliff would we spurn,
for pleasure makes one overlook the peril.[12]   14

11.

So to be Queen Camilla's[13] imitation,
(fitted, was she, with Volsci's[14] nimblest feet),
I'd dare the shepherdesses to a meet,
and reap the fruit of my swift occupation.   4
    So favored to the match were all my stars,
for with the fastest girls would I begin
and frequently surpass to dash and win,
that I'd take prize from all, and all applause.   8
    And then my hair they would adorn with garlands,
or with a shepherd's staff of gnarly myrtle,

---

[12]No other Italian woman poet has described such an experience. The author was a good horseback rider and even toyed with danger for the thrill it brought her.
[13]Virgil's woman warrior in his *Aeneid*.
[14]Camilla was queen of the Volsci and, accompanied by 300 women warriors, assisted Turnus against Aeneas.

con ferro in punta, la mia destra armaro,   11
   ed or di lauro un ramoscel frondoso,
don più d'ogni altro prezioso e caro,
di cui più che d'ogni altro è il cor bramoso.   14

12.

The nymphs Silvia and Dafne in Tasso's *Aminta* went hunting, which the author describes
with words like *tender le reti, /ed invescar le panie, ed aguzzare / il dardo ad una cote* (I, 1, lines
145–47), or *seco tendeva insidie con le reti / a i pesci ed a gli augelli* (I, 2, lines 418–19).

Il dardo e 'l veltro a l'una e a l'altra mano
talor commisi, e l'arco esercitando
al segno con lo stral l'occhio aggiustando,
non spesi il tempo e le fatiche in vano.   4
   O del rio, che sen gìa poco lontano,
con l'esca le chiar' onde conturbando,
ogni pesce prendea, ch' iva guizzando
fra l'acqua e 'l lido, semivivo e insano.   8
   O pria che uscisse il sol da l'orizonte
coi vivi raggi suoi lucenti e belli,
tesi le reti e i lacci agli altrui danni,   11
   ed ad ess' allettai gl'incauti augelli
che non temeano unquanco insidie od onte:
quinci appresi a fuggir gli umani inganni.   14

13.

The technique of listing the various elements of nature as witnesses to the poet's (or hero's)
woe was used by Petrarch in his *Valle, che de' lamenti miei se' piena* (*Rime,* CCCI). It passed on
with variants into Sannazaro's *Arcadia* and is found in sixteenth-century poets, such as Bembo,
Bandello, Tansillo and Isabella di Morra (poem VII). Turini Bufalini creates her own version,
in which her *fiumi, che al pianger mio giste più grossi* (line 6) recalls Petrarch's *fiume, che spesso
del mio pianger cresci* (CCCI, line 2).

Orride balze, cavernose grotte,
scoscesi monti, ruvinosi fossi,
che a pietà del mio duol vi siete mossi
mentre stava con voi fin a la notte.   4

with iron top, would arm my stronger hand,   11
   or sometimes make a gift of leafy laurel,
a gift to me more dear than sporting art,
the longed-for gift, most precious to my heart.[15]   14

12.

   Greyhound to one hand, to the other, arrow,
(adjusting eye on target to be slain)
I would entrust, and swiftly draw my bow,
for I did not pursue my prey in vain.[16]   4
   Then from the river just nearby, its flow
and clarity upset for my bait's gain,
I'd capture fish quivering in a throe
midst bank and stream, half-living and insane.   8
   Or when first sun upon horizon rose
with shiny rays so beautiful and bright,
snares would I set for someone's harm to meet;   11
   therein unwary birds would I enclose
that did not fear those traps and would alight:
hence did I learn to flee human deceit.   14

13.

   Oh horrid cliffs, cavernous grottoes,
ruinous gorges and craggy mountains,
you so moved to pity by my pain
while I'd remain with you till night, recluse.   4

---

[15]In spite of all the rustic Olympic victories, the author still yearns for poetic achievement.
[16]The author often went hunting with bow and arrow, and fishing and bird-catching, as well.

Acque, al mio lagrimar sonanti e rotte,
fiumi, che al pianger mio giste più grossi,
scogli, dai caldi miei sospir percossi,
onde mie voci fur spesso interrotte.   8
     Spelonche opache, altissimi dirupi,
solinghe valli, spaventosi alberghi
d'orsi feroci e di rapaci lupi.   11
     Se fia già mai, che tanto in suso io m'erghi
e ch'esca fuor di questi fondi cupi,
dei vostri onor fia che le carte io verghi.   14

14.

Se penato hai fuor del paterno tetto,
misera vita mia, fin da la cuna,
gioisci, ché propizia or tua fortuna
si volge e arreca in sen pace e diletto.   4
     Sposo d'alto valor, d'alto intelletto,
t'appresta — spoglia ormai la veste bruna,
spiega le ricche gioie ad una ad una,
e lieta te ne adorna il crine e 'l petto.   8
     Mira come è pomposo a te venuto,
ché vuol col sacro anel sua sposa farti.
Odi il cortese suo dolce saluto.   11
     T'allegra, ch' hai ragion di rallegrarti,
ché se fra i monti hai pene sostenuto,
goderai lieta in più felici parti.   14

15.

Echi, che dimorate in questi scogli
a le risposte altrui benigni, intenti,
che rispondeste al suon dei miei lamenti
mentre con voi sfogava i miei cordogli.   4
     Di Fortuna cessati or son gli orgogli,
e in pace son rivolti i miei tormenti,

Waters, who to my weeping resounded, breached;
rivers, who with my tears surged to swell high;
rocks, pounded by my torrid sighs
which oftentimes would interrupt my speech.   8
    Deepest ravines, pitch-dark lairs,
lonely valleys, frightful dens
of ravenous wolves and ferocious bears.   11
    If it may come to pass that I emerge
to sketch this underworld through ink and pen,
will I with your valor vast enrich my page.   14

14.

If from the womb you rocked in sheer distress,
my wretched life, far from paternal home,
rejoice, with favor does your Fortune turn,
your heart now with delight and peace she'll bless.   4
    With worthy groom, of high mind, does she come;
therefore, disrobe yourself of your brown dress[17]
and happily adorn your hair and breast,
display the jewels he brings you one by one.   8
    See how full of pomp he is, your swain,
for wife he wants you, with a sacred ring;
attend his greeting, his polite refrain.   11
    Be cheerful, you have every right to sing;
if, in the mountains, grief you did sustain,
you'll now taste joy in happier terrain.   14

15.

Echoes, you who make these rocks your dwelling,
to responses of those others, kind, intent,
responding to the sound of my lament
while I would vent to you, all my grief telling.   4
    To peace at last are my past torments turning,
as ceased forevermore is Fortune's pride;

---

[17]A simple brown dress was worn by women while working.

e renderete lieti i tronchi accenti,
qualor di richiamarvi il cor s'invogli.   8
    Mi parto, addio, da voi congedo piglio.
le vostre note sempre avrò nel core,
che raddolciro il mio sì duro esiglio.   11
    De la partita mia son giunte l'ore,
e porto lieto il cor, sereno il ciglio,
quanto fu mesto e torbo al mio dolore.   14

16.

    Mi parto, amiche pastorelle, e tutte
sempre nel cor vi porterò scolpite,
che pietose le mie pene infinite
più volte udiste e non con luci asciutte.   4
    Di quante volte io v'ho meco condutte
a solazzar per quell'ombre romite,
benedette sian pur l'ore gradite,
ché per voi fur le pene mie distrutte.   8
    Al vostro gregge sia propizio il Cielo,
e ogni vostro pensier conduca a riva,
né vi offenda già mai caldo né gelo.   11
    Di me sia in voi la rimembranza viva,
come io per variar fortuna e pelo,
non fia mai che di voi non canti e scriva.   14

please render light my broken words, reply,
when my heart calls you once again in yearning. 8
    Goodbye to you, I say, now I depart,
your notes I'll treasure always in my heart,
sweet tones that, with harsh exile, intervened. 11
    The hour is in reach and I must go.
I bear a heart as glad and brow serene
as each was sad and troubled at my sorrow. 14

16.

    Shepherdesses, friends, now I must leave,
yet etched forever in my heart I'll keep
you all, who would my wretched torment grieve,
you, who'd hear my pain, with me would weep. 4
    How often did I lead you out with me;
we'd play midst lonely shadows, often wander;
blest may those delightful hours be,
for by you was my suffering rent asunder. 8
    May Heaven be propitious to your fold,
and lead all of your heavy thoughts to shore,
and may you never sting from heat or cold. 11
    Let your memory of me stay a living thing,
as I, whatever Fortune has in store,
will never cease to write of you, and sing. 14

MATRIMONIO E MATERNITÀ
(1574–1582)

17.

Note that Turini Bufalini refers to her husband as *signore* (as did Colonna), and later on will also make use of the variants *consorte* and *sposo*. Also note the alternative rhyme in the *quartine*: ABAB/BABA.

A la ricca magion del mio signore
venni con bella e numerosa schiera.
Il sol mi favorì col suo splendore
ne la stagion più rigida e più fiera,   4
    ché, temprando una dolce primavera,
spuntar fe' da la terra e l'erba e 'l fiore.
Tacquero i venti a far la gioia intera,
uniti tutti al mio novello onore.   8
    E, dove il piè rivolsi, i vaghi augelli
mi salutaron con sonoro canto,
e corser chiari i torbidi ruscelli.   11
    Né di Fortuna fu lo sdegno tanto
nei trapassati dì noiosi e felli,
che non fosse il piacer poscia altretanto.   14

18.

The concluding line, *benedico il mese e 'l giorno*, is a paraphrase of Petrarch's famous verse, *benedetto sia 'l giorno, e 'l mese, et l'anno* (*Rime,* LXI, line 1).

Ampie sale, ampie logge, ampio cortile
e stanze ornate con gentil pitture,
trovai giungendo, e nobili sculture
di marmo fatte da scalpel non vile.   4
    Nobil giardin, con un perpetuo aprile
di vari fior, di frutti e di verdura,
ombre soavi, acque a temprar l'arsure,

Marriage and Motherhood

The poems in this section, **17–51**, are from *Rime* (133–65).

17.

Came I with noble retinue as escort[18]
unto my husband's house, to a rich mansion,
and though the season was most cold and hoar,
favored was I by splendor of the sun   4
    which fabricated springtime warm and sweet
and bid the earth to sprout its grass and flowers.
The winds kept still to make my ease complete;
together all conspired to do me honor.   8
    Each path I took, the birds in unison
would greet me with their song piercing the air,
while brooks would run from mud to crystal-clear.   11
    As great a rage as Fortune did employ
in bygone days, so fierce and troublesome,
so doubly great thereafter was my joy.   14

18.

Wide halls and spacious courtyards, ample loggias
and rooms all filled with paintings of fine style,
I found when first I came, and noble statues
from marble wrought by chisel never vile.[19]   4
    And in perpetual April a noble garden
of sundry flowers, of fruit and greenery,
soft shade, and water aplenty my thirst to slacken,

---

[18]A group of gentlemen on horseback that accompanied the bride to her new home.
[19]At her husband's castle in San Giustino, which had Renaissance fresco paintings and was finely decorated.

e strade di beltà non dissimile.   8
   E non men forte ostel, che per fortezza
ha il ponte e i fianchi, e lo circonda intorno
fosso profondo e di real larghezza.   11
   Qui fei col mio signor dolce soggiorno,
con santo amor, con somma contentezza,
onde ne benedico il mese e 'l giorno.   14

19.

   Vago augelin, che per quei rami ombrosi
dolce cantavi a minuir mie pene,
di sentirti al mio cor gran desir viene
per far in tutto i giorni miei giocosi.   4
   Deh, vieni e teco mena i più famosi
cantor, che quella selva in sen ritiene,
chè goderete in queste rive amene
ed a l'estivo dì starete ascosi.   8
   Il boschetto vi attende e 'l bel giardino,
là, dove in fra le fronde e l'onda e l'ôra
gareggian mormorando a me vicino.   11
   A cantar sorgeremo in sul mattino,
io, con le Muse invocherò l'Aurora,
e voi col vostro gorgheggiar divino.   14

20.

   In te, diletta mia gioconda stanza,
col mio caro signor l'ore menai;
in te la vista e 'l cor rasserenai,
non avendo più il duolo in me possanza.   4
   Riccamente vestìa, ché in abondanza
era l'aver, che in tue magion trovai,
e in avi petti un valor fu sempre mai
pregio che in terra ogn' altro pregio avanza.   8

and pathways of that very kind of beauty. 8
    And mightily strong, a castle, which for protection
has walls and bridge and for more armament
a moat so deep and vast in each direction. 11
    Here with my spouse I passed unguarded stay,
in saintly love, in plentiful content,
that I forever bless that month and day. 14

19.

    Amidst those shady branches, lovely bird,
you who sweetly sang, my pain to quell,
to hear you does desire within me stir
to fill my days with joy, make my heart swell.[20] 4
    Oh, come and bring those most renowned of singers,
all those with whom the forest's breast abounds,
for you'll be pleased with these pacific shores,
with hidden nest from summer's heat profound. 8
    This grove awaits you, and the garden lees,
the leafy treetops where the waves and breeze
compete with one another, murmuring. 11
    Arise with me at dawn if you are willing,
I, to sing Aurora[21] with my Muse
and you, as well, with your most divine trilling. 14

20.

    Room, within your dear, delightful space,
with my belovèd spouse I spent my hours;
in you my eyes, my heart found serene place,
the pain in me deprived of all its powers.[22] 4
    So richly dressed was I, for in abundance
your halls held finery beyond compare,
as elders' hearts held valor heritance,
a prize on earth that outshines every other. 8

---

[20]In spite of her happiness, there is nostalgia for the forest around Gattara, which she roamed in her youth.
[21]Goddess of dawn.
[22]Compare this poem with poem **8**. At the beginning, each represents opposite sentiments. Halfway through **20**, however, the joys have come to an end with her husband's departure for Rome, where he had military duties. The preceding calm is thus suddenly interrupted and sonnets **20–40** are all a lament for his absence.

Ma mentre mi godea sì dolce stato,
il dolce convertir fece in amaro
l'improvviso da me tôrsi da lato.   11
  Né potendo al mio duol trovar riparo,
a penar cominciai sopra ogni usato,
ché affligge il mal quanto il gioir fu caro.   14

21.

In this sonnet, the first of a series lamenting her husband's absence, the author addresses her eyes, as did Petrarch, in his *Occhi miei, oscurato è il nostro Sole* (*Rime,* CCLXXV), but she uses different words: *luci vedove* and *luci eclissate* (line 1), followed by *luci abbandonate* (line 4). She calls her husband *vivo lume* (line 2), as did Colonna.

Luci vedove mie, luci eclissate,
or che 'l mio sposo, or che 'l mio vivo lume
è partito, chi fia che più v'allume,
o mestissime luci abbandonate?   4
  S' al pianger sete avezze, al pianger nate,
com' obliando il mio natìo costume,
non riversaste allor di pianto un fiume,
che partir lo vedeste, o luci ingrate?   8
  Forse i caldi sospiri aveano asciutto
i fonti allor del lagrimoso umore,
e però non rigaste il volto e il petto?   11
  O pur gli spirti, abbandonando in tutto
voi, se n'andaro a consolar il core,
onde foste di smalto a tant' affetto?   14

22.

Come potrò già mai trovar riposo?
Anzi, come vivrò se 'l mio bel Sole,
ond' ho sol vita, il volto e le parole
m'asconde e fura, e di seguir non l'oso? 4
  Deh, riedi amante mio, riedi mio sposo,
e 'l cor che senza te si strugge e duole,

But while I lived in sweetness so adorned,
my sweetness bitter turned despite that treasure,
for from my side my love was quickly torn.   11
    Nor could I shelter grief, so robbed of pleasure,
I suffered more than ever, felt forlorn,
for grief is joy capsized, in equal measure.   14

21.

Widowed eyes of mine, you eclipsed lights,
now my spouse, my vivid flame is gone,
who will illuminate you, keep you bright,
oh eyes, you sad, you poor abandoned ones?   4
    If used to weeping and to crying born,
as if forgetting my accustomed plight,
how did you not a flume of tears pour down,
ungrateful eyes that saw him out of sight?   8
    The very heat, perhaps, of my warm sighing
had dried the source where springs of tears must start,
so on my face and breast no bright drops shone.   11
    Or else I think at once my spirits, flying,
abandoned you to go console the heart,
so that, despite great love, you turned to stone.   14

22.

However will I now recover peace?
How will I live, if my beautiful Sun[23]
who grants to me my life, my words, my face,
hides, flees where I dare never follow him?   4
    Come back to me, my love, come back, my spouse,
so that my heart that pines for you in pain,

---

[23]Metaphor for her husband.

e 'l cor, che senza te né può né vuole
viver, col lume tuo rendi gioioso.   8
    O mira almen che la tua fida ancella
ti va cercando con aperte braccia,
se pur ti trovi in questa parte e in quella.   11
    Deh, scopri a me la tua serena faccia,
e sentir fammi il suon di tua favella,
se non vuoi che per pianto io mi disfaccia.   14

23.

The intonation of this poem and the use of *crudel*, both as a noun (line 1) and as an adjective
(line 14), are typical of seventeenth-century musical songs, although used before by other
poets, as by Tasso, in a sonnet, *Crudel, se tu non credi a' miei lamenti* (*Rime,* 355, line 1), and in
a madrigal (*Rime,* 467, line 4).

    Crudel, che del mio mal nulla tu curi,
ed hai d'aspe l'orecchia ai miei lamenti.
Già commossi a pietà de' miei tormenti
si fan molti i macigni, e tu t'induri.   4
    Ahi, chi fia mai che 'l mio dolor misuri,
chi a noverar i miei sospiri ardenti
prenda, e l'umor di questi occhi correnti
che son già fatti nubilosi e scuri.   8
    Da' suoi profondi abissi Eco risponde
al mio doglioso strido, e i vaghi augelli
fanno a gara i lamenti e le querele.   11
    Dolce mormora l'aura in fra le fronde,
piangon pietosi e limpidi i ruscelli,
tu sol sei sordo, idol mio crudele.   14

24.

Note the alternative rhyme in the *quartine*: ABAB/BABA.

    Forse mosso a pietà de' miei lamenti
e del pianto, ch' irriga e 'l volto e 'l seno,

so that my heart without you will not cease;
joyful make my heart leap with your flame.   8
    Or see at least that your most faithful wife
with open arms awaits you ever trying
to find you here or there, in every place.   11
    Oh, show from out this hiding your calm face
and let me hear your voice so that from crying
I will not be undone; I will have life.   14

23.

    Cruel one, you care nothing for my torture;
like asps', your ears are blocked to my laments.
Moved far more to pity by my torments
is any rock or stone, yet you grow harder.   4
    Oh, who might of my pain take ample measure,
who number my sighs for you so ardent,
fathom tears from eyes in weeping spent,
eyes now rendered cloudy and obscure?   8
    From deep abyss Echo answers my cry again,
and lovely birds to multiply my grief
compete with one another, cry, complain.   11
    The breezes murmur softly leaf to leaf,
rivulets mourn in pitiful refrain,
but only you, my idol cruel, are deaf.   14

24.

    Perhaps imbued with pity for my cries,
and for my tears which flood my face and breast,

ha d'atre nubi al sole i rai lucenti
velati 'l ciel, già chiaro or d'orror pieno.　　　　4
　　E di sì largo umor bagna 'l terreno,
che turba ai rivi i liquefatti argenti,
ma in breve spazio l'orror suo vien meno,
sol gli occhi miei son fiumi ognor correnti.　　8
　　Occhi miei senza luce, in alto orrore,
petto mio, solo di mestizia albergo,
cor senz' alma, alma sol viva al dolore,　　　11
　　in van, ahimè, voi v'affliggete, io vergo
le carte in van, le carte, ohimè, ch'amore
fa che di pianto e non d'inchiostro aspergo.　　14

25.

Compare Turini Bufalini's lines 1–4 to Poliziano's *Avea fatto al suo nido già ritorno / la stanca rondinella peregrina* (*Stanze per la giostra*, 25, lines 3–4) or Tasso's *Tu parti, o rondinella, e poi ritorni / pur d'anno in anno, e fai la state il nido* (*Rime*, 207, lines 1–2).

Rondinella gentil, tu fai ritorno,
tosto che passa 'l verno e april rimena
l'alma stagion sì florida ed amena,
a fare al nido tuo dolce soggiorno.　　　　4
　　Ma 'l mio signor del suo venire il giorno
non trova e scior non sa l'aspra catena,
per lui son ghiacci e nevi e non serena
il tempo e fremon venti orridi intorno.　　8
　　Tornano i vaghi fior, tornan gli augelli,
verdeggia 'l prato, la campagna e 'l bosco,
corron sonanti e limpidi i ruscelli.　　　11
　　Ma solo è il viver mio penoso e fosco,
e vano egli è ch'io il mio signor rappelli,
e pasco il cor di doloroso tosco.　　　　14

so paint with dread their clearest hues, the skies,
with veils of clouds midst lucent sun, suppressed.   4
    And with such humor[24] drench the earth, oppressed,
disturb the streams where liquid silver[25] plies;
at once, though, downpour's horror comes to rest,
but not the constant river from my eyes.   8
    Eyes of mine in darkness, in great dread,
breast of mine, to utter sadness hostel,
heart less soul, where pain abides, soul–dead,   11
    in vain, alas, you grieve. I write and wrestle
with pen on page to tell my love; instead,
my tears, not ink, there flow from its deep well.   14

25.

    Peaceful swallow, like sojourning guest,
when April enters, just at winter's end,
with such a flowery and delightful season,
then you return to stay in your dear nest.   4
    My lord, though, his return he cannot wrest;
he cannot find a way to break his chains;
he finds but ice and snow, not sky serene,
and horrid winds he fights, and sheer tempest.   8
    The lovely flowers bloom, birds reappear,
the fields, the hills, the woods to green revert,
and all the brooks run sonorous and clear.   11
    My life alone turns darker and distraught;
in vain I call my lord; he cannot hear,
so I with plaintive poison feed my heart.   14

---

[24]Humidity, liquid, or water — here rain.
[25]Metaphor for the clear, silvery color of the water of the stream.

26.

In describing spring, the author follows the Italian poetic tradition. Her line 10 is taken from Petrarch, *ogni animal d'amar si riconsiglia* (*Rime*, CCCX, line 8).

Ecco la dolce e vaga primavera,
che spunta il giglio e la vermiglia rosa,
l'aria soave e l'alba rugiadosa
del bel lucido sol nunzia primiera.   4
    Verdeggia il prato e i pesci, a schiera a schiera,
guizzan fra l'onde; ecco la selva ombrosa,
Filomena garrir dolce e pietosa,
girar tepido il sol l'aurata sfera,   8
    corron sonanti e cristallini umori,
ogni animal d'amar si riconsiglia,
inghirlandati van ninfe e pastori.   11
    Del dolce tempo ognun letizia piglia,
sol io non scemo il mio mortal dolore,
né già mai posso serenar le ciglia.   14

27.

The enamored fish, that *guizzano* and perform *balli* (lines 3–4), recall Poliziano's description of his *muti pesci* that *guidon felice e dilettoso ballo … un po' guizzando* (*Stanze per la giostra*, 89). The enumeration of various natural elements that follows, a device typical of the late Cinquecento and early Seicento, was used to indicate that the suffering and tears of the poet were even greater. This theme derives from Petrarch's *Non à tanti animali il mar fra l'onde* (*Rime*, CCXXXVII). Note the alternative rhyme in the *quartine*: ABAB/BABA.

Mentre del Tebro i liquefatti argenti
corron sonanti e per gli obliqui calli
guizzano i pesci un contro l'altro ardenti,
ché guida Amor ne l'acque anco i suoi balli,   4
    su le rive, di fior vermigli e gialli
sparse e d'erbette e degli umor sorgenti,
m'assido, e al suon de' limpidi cristalli
accordo i lagrimosi miei lamenti.   8
    Tanti pesci non ha questo o quel gorgo,
né tante frondi e fior le sponde amene,

26.

Here comes the spring, so beautiful and new,
sprouting the lily and vermilion rose;
the gentle air and dawn's refreshing dew
announce themselves as sun's first messengers;   4
   and verdant meadow, fish so numerous
who wriggle through the waves. In forest's mew
trills Philomela,[26] softly dolorous;
warm rays of sun their golden spheres pursue;   8
   the streams run babbling and crystalline,
and amorous turns every animal;
on nymphs' and shepherds' brows garlands entwine.   11
   All celebrate the weather's balm so fine;
but I, my mortal grief I cannot quell,
nor will my brow, my eyes, cease to repine.   14

27.

While Tiber's[27] waters run like liquid silver,[28]
bubbling through such crooked narrow straits,
and fish swim ardently one next the other,
for Love guides their dance, too, of mate to mate,   4
   nearby these liquid springs, on grass I sit,
on banks bedecked with red and yellow flower;
I match lament and, sobbing, weep my fate
alone, unto the sound of limpid water.   8
   No whirlpool here holds fish in any measure,
nor do these banks show count of bud or leaf,

---

[26]Represents the nightingale. Philomela and her sister, Procne, were changed, respectively, into a nightingale and a swallow, after they killed Itys, son of Procne and Tereus, Procne's husband, because Tereus had raped Philomela.

[27]The Tiber River, which originates in Tuscany, flows through Umbria, not far from San Giustino and Città di Castello, near the possessions of the Bufalini family.

[28]The silvery water of the river.

quante lagrime allor dagli occhi sgorgo.　　　　　11
　　Tante il lido non ha minute arene,
né mover tante foglie al vento scorgo,
che non sian più le mie gravose pene.　　　　　14

28.

　　Passato è 'l verno, nuvoloso e fiero,
con notti oscure, all'uom noiose tanto,
con piogge e neve e ghiaccio in ogni canto,
negando il sole il suo calore intiero.　　　　　4
　　Tornato è 'l maggio di bei fiori altiero,
rivestito ha la terra il verde manto,
e i già muti augellin, svegliati al canto,
destan le fere al lor amor primiero.　　　　　8
　　E voi pastor, che 'l gregge allontanaste,
or che l'erbette i campi han rivestito,
tornate ai cari monti, che lasciaste.　　　　　11
　　Solo a me resta ogni pensier schernito,
chè 'l mutare stagion non è che baste,
perché a me torni il mio signor gradito.　　　　　14

29.

The theme of seeing the beloved person in a dream originates with Petrarch (*Rime*, CCCII), and was used by the Petrarchists.

　　Entro un ombroso speco a l'ombra fresca,
ove corre un bel rio con rotto accento,
chiaro via più che liquefatto argento,
che, mormorando, a udir l'anima invesca,　　　　　4
　　dormiva allor, ché par che l'ora incresca
quando 'l sol più riscalda e tace il vento,
per dar qualche ristauro al mio tormento,
e 'l cor pascea di nobilissim' esca.　　　　　8
　　Quando venirmi avanti a l'improvviso
vidi il mio sposo con serena faccia,

as do my eyes produce their wealth of tears.   11
    And moving leaves in number are much briefer,
and grains of sand count less upon this shore,
than does my sum of troubles, weight of grief.   14

28.

    Gone are the clouds and fiercest cold of winter,
with nights so dark and foul for everyone,
each crevice filled with ice and snow and rain,
the sun denying us its warmth entire.   4
    The month of May returns, proud of its flowers,
to dress the earth again in mantle green,
and birds once silent, now on singing keen,
awaken all beasts to loves of before.   8
    Shepherds, who from high pasture led your flocks,
now new grass blankets every field and lee,
you seek again those dear peaks that you left.   11
    But I find every thought a mockery,
for change in season will not be enough
to bring my welcome lord back home to me.[29]   14

29.

    Under the cooling shadow of shady cavern,
where runs a pretty brook with broken sounds,
clearer than silver, its murmur to discern,
enticing the soul to tend as it expounds,   4
    I slept through time of day that most concerns,
when sun is warmest and no wind resounds;
on noble bait I fed my heart, to lure,
with thought to find some respite from my wounds.   8
    When suddenly I saw before me there
my spouse as he appears with his calm face:

---

[29]This is the last poem in the 1627 edition of *Rime*. The 1628 edition is identical to this point, then simply continues with new poems, starting with our sonnet **29**.

dicendo: "ecco al venir c'ho sciolto il laccio."   11
    Mentre al collo gettar gli vo' le braccia,
non sapendo s'in terra o in paradiso
fossi, l'ombra sparisce e l'aura abbraccio.   14

30.

    Qualor, per far men grave 'l mio tormento,
muovo le piante al nobil giardino,
che il palagio real di San Giustino
cinge con ammirabile ornamento,   4
    sì dolce pianger Filomena io sento,
ch'a udir mi fermo il canto pellegrino,
e mentre gli occhi lagrimando inchino,
di pianto aspergo ambe le guance e il mento,   8
    ché mi sovvien di te, grand'alma, ond'io
spargo dai lumi inessicabil vena,
e con gli accenti sfogo il dolor mio.   11
    Ch'onde sperai d'alleggerir mia pena,
gli augei, le piante e 'l gorgogliar del rio
"Piangi," dicon, "né 'l pianto mai raffrena."   14

31.

    Torna, Sol di quest'occhi, almo e sereno,
e sgombra il ghiaccio e 'l tempestoso verno;
già il cor mio rode un rio timor interno,
forse che altra beltà t'ingombra il seno.   4
    Se non vuoi che dal duolo io venga meno,
tu, della nave tua torna al governo,
ch'in tanta lontananza io ben discerno
che per me sol di noia il mondo è pieno.   8
    Se ben di tua bontà molto mi fido,
pur fredda tema, ohimè, figlia d'Amore,
m'induce al cor sospetti iniqui e rei.   11
    Torna, ardente mio Sol, torna al tuo nido,

"Here, broken are the chains of my homecoming." 11
    My arms around his neck I yearn to fling,
confused if bound to earth or Paradise
I be; but then he's gone. I embrace air. 14

30.

    At times, to make less grave my woes incessant,
I turn my steps to wander in the garden
which rings the royal palace of San Giustino
with admirable skill and ornament. 4
    Philomela's plaintive cry I hear therein,
and to her unique song I pause to listen,
incline my weeping eyes where my tears glisten
cascading down to bathe my cheeks and chin, 8
    because, great soul, of you I'm ever thinking,
my eyes spill tears from never-ending vein,
and words pour forth to beg from grief release. 11
    But even if I hope to lessen pain,
the birds, the plants, the river's murmuring,
to me say, "Cry, and never let tears cease." 14

31.

    Return, Sun of my eyes, calm and serene,
and clear away the ice and stormy winter;
there gnaws inside my heart an evil fear,
a different beauty steals you, unforeseen. 4
    If you don't want to have my death to mourn,
return to guide your ship, take hold the rudder,
for I know trouble finds me, and no other;
across this distance, that much I discern. 8
    Although your faithfulness I greatly trust,
an icy dread, alas, daughter of Love,
makes wickedest suspicions fill my breast. 11
    Return, my fiery Sun, to your dear nest,

ché, s'otterrà mai tanta pace il core,
più non ti disciorrai dai lacci miei.   14

32.

Sarà già mai che tant' aspra durezza
del tuo gelido cor rompa 'l mio pianto;
sarà già mai, che mi conduca a tanto,
che pari a tua beltà veggia fermezza?   4
     O de l'anima mia pace e dolcezza,
come lunge da me puoi viver tanto?
Deh, godiam l'amor nostro onesto e santo,
e la cara union che sì s'apprezza.   8
     Crudel, che pensi a che indugiando vai?
Forse attendi oltra il cor la mia persona?
Oh, se 'l potessi far, come 'l farei,   11
     ma col pensiero almen, che sì mi sprona,
sempre son teco, e ben t'è noto ormai,
ma tu sei sordo ai preghi, ai pianti miei.   14

33.

Se per aver del travaglioso giorno
qualche quiete a la mia vita greve,
mi corco, oh, quanto quel riposo è breve
e quanto è presto il sol a far ritorno.   4
     E ben che i raggi suoi scopra d'intorno,
non è però ch'il mio dolor disgreve,
anzi desta a me par che più s'aggreve,
e bramo il ciel veder di stelle adorno.   8
     Che far debb'io, se 'l dì, né men la notte,
non ho quiete e non ho pace alcuna;
Morte, almen trammi dalla vita fore.   11
     Posano gli animai ne le lor grotte;
debb'io sola penar, crudel Fortuna,
tal premio dassi a un sì fedele amore?   14

for if my heart with that much peace be blest,
free from my snares again you'll never leave.   14

32.

    Will the day come when tears of mine will break
the hard-heartedness of your icy core?
Will the day come when your good looks will take
a place equal in you with staying power?   4
    Oh, my soul's peace and joy, do not forsake
our love. Why live so long from me, so far?
Oh, let's enjoy our union for love's sake,
our saintly, honest love that we hold dear.   8
    What are you thinking, cruel one? Why delay?
If I could transport not just soul, but self
to you, I'd gladly come, I need not say.   11
    At least my thoughts go always forth, and they,
as you well know, keep me not far away,
but to my tears, my prayers, you are deaf.   14

33.

    If, to escape the travail of my hours,
to find some peace for my burdensome life,
I go to bed, oh, how that rest is brief
and how soon sun returns, as though not far.   4
    And even as the sun unveils its rays,
I cannot seem to find decrease of grief;
instead, awake, I've pain without relief,
and I desire to see the sky with stars.   8
    What shall I do, if neither day nor night,
I find no peace at all, no end to plight;
at least remove me from this life, oh Death.   11
    While animals in grottoes find respite,
just I, cruel Fortune, suffer; is it right
to honor so a love that had such faith?   14

34.

Sognando stendo or l'uno, or l'altro braccio,
ch'il mio Sol veder sembra a l'alma insana,
e 'l chiuso speco e la nud' ombra vana,
sospirando e piangendo indarno abbraccio.   4
    Come la neve al sol, così mi sfaccio,
sgorgando da questi occhi una fontana,
e dico come l'allegrezza umana
è breve e senza fin lungo l'impaccio.   8
    A far doppio il mio mal come t'appresti,
Fortuna ria, con questo finto oggetto,
perché 'l mio duol ogn'altro duolo avanzi?   11
    Lungi, lungi da me fantasmi infesti,
fugga la frode il pastoral ricetto
e sol ne l'empio inferno alberghi e stanzi.   14

35.

The author invites nature to cry with her and creates almost an Arcadian motif. The expression, *segretarie antiche* (line 10), is derived from Petrarch's … *quel dolce pensero / che secretario antico è* … (*Rime,* CLXVIII, lines 1–2).

Lieto boschetto alteramente adorno
di verdi abeti e d'odorati allori,
ov'a sfogar i miei gravi dolori,
così per tempo solitaria torno.   4
    L'aria soave e l'armonia, ch'in torno
forman gli augelli ai mattutini albori,
e 'l mormorio dei cristallini umori
mi lusingan a far con voi soggiorno.   8
    E dico: oh care e fortunate piante,
de le mie pene segretarie antiche,
sentite 'l suon de le mie note amare.   11
    Augelli, voi ch'in un con l'aura errante
meco piangete e voi chiar' onde amiche,
col pianto mio date tributo al mare.   14

34.

One arm and now the other I extend
sleeping, for my sick soul sees again
my Sun; this cave, bare shade thus imagined
while sighing, crying, I embrace in vain.[30]   4
    I melt away as snow does in the sun,
and from these shedding eyes a fountain runs;
I say that joyfulness when it be human
is short, and human trouble without end.   8
    Oh wicked Fortune, how you seem to boast
in doubling pain with visions insubstantial
so that my suffering's a double hell.   11
    Away, away from me you harmful ghosts;
let fraud flee from this shelter pastoral[31]
and in evil inferno lodge and dwell.   14

35.

Lovely little woods, amply adorned
with firs so green, with laurels' spicy odor,
where to give vent to my grief and my dolor,
I turn so early on, and so alone.   4
    The soft air and the sweet harmonious tune
that birds in white of morning make with ardor,
the murmuring of your crystalline humors[32]
entice me ever with you to sojourn.   8
    I ask you, my dear plants so fortunate,
you ancient secret-keepers of my plaint,
to listen to my notes so bitter truly.   11
    Oh, birds and breeze, together, cry with me;
and you, clear, friendly waves, with my lament,
with tears of mine pay tribute to the sea.   14

---

[30]This poem is a variant of the theme of poem **29**, where the author describes falling asleep in a cave. The same is true here, for otherwise she could not embrace "the cave."
[31]Peaceful place.
[32]Water.

36.

For the theme of Echo see comments to poem **4**.

Eco risponde ai miei dogliosi accenti
e tu, che dolce sì tra questi rami,
garrula Filomena, a te richiami
l'antico duol, t'accordi a miei lamenti.   4
    Rivi e voi, che gemendo ite, correnti
cresciuti al pianto di quest' occhi grami,
e s'entro voi v'è qualche ninfa ch'ami,
piangete insieme i gravi miei tormenti.   8
    Aure soavi e voi fere selvagge,
pendete al suon de l'alte mie querele,
al suon che spargo ognor per queste piagge,   11
    poiché Fortuna, a me sempre crudele,
mi vieta che le note amate e sagge
non oda più de l'idol mio fedele.   14

37.

This Petrarchist sonnet recalls the first four lines of the master's *Quel rosignuol che sì soave piange* (*Rime*, CCCXI, lines 1–4), but is expressed with different words, while the *passi tardi e lenti* (line 8), are Petrarch's (*Rime*, XXXV, line 2). Note the alternative rhyme in the *quartine*: ABAB/BABA.

Dolce usignuol, che con soavi accenti
lagrimi forse la perduta sposa,
l'antico mio dolor tu mi rammenti,
con la tremula tua voce amorosa.   4
    Ma s'io d'amare stille rugiadosa
porto la guancia e faccio udir lamenti,
e dove veggo più la selva ombrosa
ne vo piangendo a passi tardi e lenti,   8
    non però impetro agl'indurati affetti
tregua, e tu, pur con le tue note sole,
le fere e i sassi ad ascoltarti alletti.   11
    Ma s'uguali al dolor le mie parole

36.

Echo answers now my doleful accents,
and you, who midst these branches sing again,
garrulous Philomela, your past pain,
you harmonize your song to my laments. 4
    Waters, and you who run by wailing, currents
swollen with the tears of eyes that mourn,
if there be with you nymph who loves, bemoan
oh nymph and waters, my most woeful torments. 8
    Soft wind, and you, beasts of the wilderness,
bend to the sound of my extreme complaints,
the sound that to these banks I must address, 11
    since Fortune, always cruel with me, prevents
that those wise words, belovèd, eloquent
of my true idol I might list, and rest. 14

37.

Sweet nightingale, with your gentle refrain
you weep, perhaps, for your departed spouse,
and bring me back again to my old pain,
with tremulous voice of yours so amorous. 4
    But I let bitter drops pour down my face,
with dewy cheeks I let lament be plain,
and I go cry, at slow and tardy pace,
within the woods where shadows hold their reign. 8
    Yet I obtain for my hardened affliction
no truce, where you, instead, just with your trill
entice both beasts and stones until all harken. 11
    But if my words to my harsh pain were equal,

fossero, spererei negli altrui petti
destar pietate e far fermar il sole.   14

38.

Vaghi cespugli di pupuree rose,
prati dipinti e voi siepi fiorite,
aure, che il lor odor mi compartite,
mitigate le mie pene gravose.   4
Pastorelle dolcissime amorose,
che 'l pianto mio, ch' i miei lamenti udite,
temprate 'l duol de l'aspre mie ferite,
né siate al pregar mio sorde e ritrose.   8
Eco, che sì pietosa mi rispondi,
poscia ch'al mio chiamar sord' è la Morte,
mesci 'l tuo duol co' miei sospir profondi.   11
O se tutto è contrario a la mia sorte,
siatemi almeno per pietà secondi,
voi, chiari spirti de l'empirea corte.   14

39.

O Fortuna crudel, non sazia a pieno
di avermi il mio signor tolto da lato,
depor m'hai fatto il parto desiato,
anzi stagion, di che avea grave il seno.   4
Sento il cor per gran duol venirsi meno,
e se vuol pur ch'io pera iniquo fato,
questo estremo contento a me sia dato,
ch'io lo riveggia anzi ch'io mora almeno.   8
Questi son i trionfi e le dolcezze
che attendea del bramato tuo ritorno,
che n'abbia a scompagnar tant' amarezze?   11
Mi duol nel fin non ti aver d'intorno,
vieni se 'n vita di vedermi apprezze.
Non indugiar, che se n' tramonta il giorno.   14

I'd hope inside the hearts of everyone
some pity to awake, make sun stand still.   14

38.

   Purple rosebush with your loveliness,
painted meadows and you, hedge in bloom,
breezes that blow to me such perfume,
lighten for me pain that does oppress.   4
   Sweet and loving, every shepherdess
unto my crying, my laments, attuned,
temper the distress of my harsh wounds,
and to my plight, entreaty, be not deaf.   8
   Echo, full of pity, you respond,
where, deafened to my calling, Death comes not;
combine your sadness with my sighs profound.   11
   If all must be contrary to my lot,
for pity's sake, stay with me, stay around,
you sprightly spirits of the heavenly court.   14

39.

   Oh Fortune cruel, why do you never rest
with having my love from me ever torn?
Too soon, you took my hoped-for child, stillborn
and premature; you plucked him from my breast.[33]   4
   I feel my heart with so much grief may cease.
If, evil Fate, you want my days to end,
I beg that this last wish to me you send:
I'll see my lord before I die, at least.   8
   Are these the triumphs and the sweet sojourn
that I foresaw from your[34] longed-for return,
that I will share with bitter, inner strife?   11
   Without you at my side I am in pain;
come, if you care to see me yet in life.
Do not delay; day sets beyond the mountain.   14

---

[33]The author lost her first baby prematurely, while her husband was away, and she almost died from fever, as she relates in poem **40**.
[34]The author now addresses her husband.

40.

Ardente febbre mi consuma il core,
e doppia sete togliemi il riposo:
una di veder te, dolce mio sposo,
l'altra causata dal maligno ardore.   4
    Né so dir de le due qual sia maggiore,
o quella ond' il pensiero è desioso,
o quella ond'ho 'l cor mesto e desioso
d'un chiaro fonte di agghiacciato umore.   8
    De l'acqua pur talor mi riconforto,
de la vista di amico e di congiunto,
che con men duol il mal fan, ch'io sopporto.   11
    E s'a me non arrivi in spazio corto,
il fin dei giorni miei sent'esser giunto,
né vivo il corpo mio vedrai, né morto.   14

41.

Torna, caro mio ben, ché viva ancora
pur son, che non credea. M'oppresse il male
l'alma così che al ciel spiegava l'ale,
già giunta al fin di sua mortal dimora.   4
    Come ti veggio d'ogni mal son fuora,
però se 'l viver mio punto ti cale,
col venir vederò se 'l pregar vale,
ch'in tua man sta ch'io viva o pur ch'io mora.   8
    Se sapess' il dolor che mi tormenta:
esser lungi da te priva del figlio,
il mio martir la faccia rappresenta.   11
    Oscurato è quasi il seren del ciglio,
tu ravvivar puoi la mia speme spenta
e trarmi fuor di noia e di periglio.   14

40.

My heart is eaten up by burning fire.
I lose my sleep to greedy double thirst:
the one, of seeing you again, sweet sire,
the other, killing fever as the source.   4
    Nor can I tell which of the two is first,
the wished-for thing to which my mind aspires,
or icy water from the fountain clearest,
often the thing my saddened heart desires.   8
    At times, to comfort me, I take some water,
or have in sight a friend or relative,
which makes the pain a bit more light to bear.   11
    But if you fail with due speed to arrive,
as ending of my days I feel draws near,
you'll see my body neither dead nor live.   14

41.

Return, dearly belov'd, I am alive
though I thought not. The illness so oppressed
my soul that I spread out my wings to fly,
my soul nearly run through its mortal test.   4
    When I see you, danger will pass, I'll rest,
so if you care at all that I revive,
make toil of my imploring manifest;
it's in your hands if I will live or die.   8
    If you but knew the pain I must embrace:
so far from you, and deprived of my son,
my suffering's reflected in my face.   11
    My eyes' serenity has been erased;
extinguished, hope returns with you alone;
my troubles and my peril, come, displace.   14

42.

Se le promesse di tornar forz' hanno,
che m'han da mort' in vita ritornato,
che sarà quando rivedrotti, amato
mio sposo, in cui le mie speranze stanno.   4
    Del mal più non avrò tema né danno,
il ciglio e 'l cor vedrai rasserenato,
le Muse torneranno al canto usato
che smarrite or da me lungi sen vanno.   8
    E in vece di sospiri, di amari lai,
lieta ritornerò, qual star solea,
se 'l mancar di tua fè non leggier fai.   11
    Con questa speme il cor mio si ricrea,
e l'ore conto che indugiando vai,
già ti veggio appressar ne la mia idea.   14

43.

Cor mio, ch'in pianto hai trapassato l'ore,
menando mesta e solitaria vita,
da che l'acerba e dura dipartita
fece da te l'amato tuo signore.   4
    L'allegrezza or raddoppi il tuo dolore,
del suo ritorno che ti porge aita:
ecco la luce già da te sparita
che t'alluma col sol del suo splendore.   8
    Corrigli incontro con aperte braccia,
stringilo, prendi l'onorata mano,
pasci la vista in rimirar sua faccia.   11
    Ascolta il suo parlar soave e piano,
ed ogni duolo, ogni timor discaccia,
ché più non sogni e più nol chiami in vano.   14

42.

If to your promises to come you hold,
which bring me back again from death to life,
how will I be when I see you, belovèd
spouse, in whom all hope lies for your wife.   4
     I'll have no fear of illness, as of old.
My eyes, my heart, will light with love, be rife.
The Muses will let song in me unfold,
for now they vanish from me, lost to grief.   8
     No bitter lays, no tears, will I then weep,
but filled with joy I'll be, of the same kind
as I once was, if to your pledge you keep.   11
     With this one hope my heart its peace will find.
Oh, how the hours between us seem to creep;
I see you there approaching, in my mind.   14

43.

     My heart, you wanted nothing but to grieve,
to lead a life so lonesome and so sad,
the moment that your most belovèd lord
deprived you with his hard and bitter leave.   4
     At his return, and help that he will offer,
may twice your pain be joy you now receive:
here is the light that he did from you cleave,
that now shines on you the sun of its splendor.   8
     Run quickly to him with your open arms,
take up his honored hand, give him embrace,
and feast your eyes in gazing at his face,   11
     and listen to his words, gentle and calm,
that chase away all of your fear, all pain.
No longer must you dream, or call in vain.[35]

---

[35]Sonnets **43–48** describe the poet's happiness after her husband's return.

44.

Giorno felice, desiato giorno,
ora propizia, fortunato punto,
ché 'l mio bel Sole agli occhi nostri è giunto
per cui tant' arse il cor del suo ritorno.   4
   Quanto piansi e penai di giorno in giorno,
il cor festeggerà col suo cor giunto,
ed a tanto giorir sia questo aggiunto
che da me non più involi il viso adorno.   8
   Se piangeste, occhi miei, or ben dovete
serenarvi e mirar lieti e gioiosi
lui, che tanto veder bramato avete.   11
   Ma che tanti scritto hai versi dogliosi,
timida, or che non hai chi te lo vieti,
stringer lo sposo tuo forse non osi.   14

45.

Dopo una lunga ed orrida tempesta,
torna sereno il ciel, scopresi 'l sole.
Dopo l'inverno i gigli e le viole
spuntano fuor con odorosa vesta.   4
   Tal io, dopo 'l languir doglioso e mesta
lungi dal ben, cui l'alma adora e cole,
or, a sua vista, al suon di sue parole,
torno felice, in dolce gioia e in festa.   8
   E se già piansi e sospirai cotanto,
la notte e 'l dì, bramando il suo ritorno,
or viverò tranquilla in riso e in canto.   11
   È giunto pur quel fortunato giorno,
qual fa l'indugio il ben dolce altretanto,
tal fia seco più dolce il mio soggiorno.   14

44.

Happy day, day so long in wait,
oh lucky moment in this hour propitious,
my lovely Sun is restored to our eyes,
for whose return so burned my fevered heart.   4
    My heart, conjoined with his, will celebrate,
and may this wish be added to my bliss,
that never more he hide from me his face
for which, day upon day, I cried, distraught.   8
    If once you cried, my eyes, you must turn clear,
and take a gladdened and a joyous look
at him, the sight of whom you prayed appear.   11
    But since so many mournful rhymes you wrote,
oh timid one, though no one holds you back,
to now embrace your spouse, you may dare not.   14

45.

When horrifying storm has come and gone,
the sky returns serene, the sun is met
at winter's end with lilies, violets
that sprout to make the earth's most fragrant gown.   4
    So I once separate mourned, but since have found
my love, whom I adore and venerate,
and I turn happy, festive, joyful, sweet
at sight of him, his voice, his words, their sound.   8
    And if I cried and sighed so much, so long,
both night and day awaiting his return,
now I'll live peacefully, with smiles, with song.   11
    The happy day has come for which I yearned,
which makes delay a blessing just as strong;
so sweeter with him will be my sojourn.   14

46.

Reo, ch'agli occhi abbia già la benda negra,
il laccio al collo ed al supplizio appresso,
se "grazia" ode gridar, non più s'allegra
di quel ch'a me fu di gioir permesso.   4
    Né legno da procella infida ed egra,
agitato ne l'alto e quasi oppresso,
giunse in porto già mai con gioia integra
pari a la gioia ond'io provai l'eccesso,   8
    quando vidi il mio Sol dopo tanti anni
tornar a me col suo giocondo viso,
ch' è più soave il ben dopo gli affanni.   11
    Era dal sen lo spirto ormai diviso,
e se 'l duol non mi diè gli ultimi danni,
quasi fu dal diletto il cor ucciso.   14

47.

Desiri ardenti, brame sitibonde,
occhi che umor versaste in larga vena,
che fate, or che la faccia, alma e serena,
mirate e che i suoi rai più non v'asconde?   4
    Mostrate or, con voci alme e feconde,
che fuggita è del cor l'antica pena,
e quanto è di piacer l'alma ripiena
in riveder le luci alme gioconde.   8
    De la sua assenza il sostenuto duolo,
l'eloquenza s'adopri a dispiegare,
sì che l'arresti a non spiegar più il volo;   11
    con catene d'Amor convien legare,
ché la via quest' è a ritenerlo solo,
su, su, timido cor, ch'indugi a fare?   14

46.

Upon the scaffold, neck by the noose ringed,
a culprit, black cloth tied about his eyes,
if executioner his "pardoned" cries,
is not more glad than I, now I can sing.   4
    Nor could a ship, by tempest blustering,
tossed up and almost crushed, ever surmise
to reach its port with joyous enterprise
equal to joy I felt, astonishing,   8
    to see my Sun, held back so many years[36]
and with his cheerful face now in my sight,
for sweeter is the good after the sighs.   11
    My spirit from my breast almost took flight,
and if past pain did not bring my demise,
my heart was nearly slain by my delight.   14

47.

Avid longings, amorous desires,
eyes that in large veins[37] shed ample tears,
what are you doing, now that you can gaze
at his divine, calm face and all its rays?   4
    Show him, with words divine, made to inspire,
the soul that now resides so full of pleasure,
the heart that banished its pain of past days
in seeing his eyes so divine and gay.   8
    The suffering endured with his departure
may eloquence endeavor to display,
so that he'll not fly off again, but stay.   11
    With chains of love you must tie him secure,
to hold him here, that is the only way;
on, on, shy heart, why do you so delay?   14

---

[36]Francesca married in 1574. She had a miscarriage before her husband returned. Her son, Giulio, was born in 1576 so her husband must have been away for about a year only.
[37]In abundance.

48.

Per le gioconde stanze e ornate sale,
per l'ampie logge e 'l florido giardino,
vattene lieta al tuo signor vicino,
in ricompensa del passato male.   4
    La gioia tua non ha dolcezza uguale:
questo palagio altier, tuo pellegrino
Parnaso è divenuto almo e divino
de le Muse, con festa universale.   8
    Danzan le ninfe amorosetti balli,
ghirlandate di rose e di viole,
teco nei prati e per l'ombrose valli.   11
    Ti favorisce il ciel, la terra e 'l sole,
e dove vai per fortunati calli
ti risponde Eco in musiche parole.   14

49.

O desiato mio diletto e caro
figlio, o viva del cor speme gradita,
e negli affanni miei fatale aita,
o dì sempre per me celebre e chiaro.   4
    Benedetto quel duol senza riparo,
c'ho sostenuto nel donarti vita.
O come in segno c'ha mia voce udita,
mi ha fatto 'l Ciel eccelso dono e raro.   8
    Vivi, caro mio ben, e teco viva
mia vita istessa e del tuo padre augusto
la stanca speme in te ritorni viva.   11
    E s'esser brami e saggio e forte e giusto,
ne la memoria eternamente avviva
degli avi tuoi l'alto splendor vetusto.   14

48.

Through all the ornate halls and cheerful rooms,[38]
through loggias wide and garden fresh in bloom,
go happily to be beside your lord,
as recompense for past harm is assured.   4
    Your joy now can be equal to no other:
these noble palace walls in which you wander
are sacred turned into divine Parnassus
where Muses sing in universal feast.   8
    The nymphs with rose and violet are crowned,
and dance with you their most amorous dance
amid the shady valleys and the meadows.   11
    All favor you — the sky, the earth, the sun —
and as upon auspicious paths you prance,
with words most musical Echo ensues.   14

49.[39]

Oh long-awaited, dear, belovèd son,[40]
oh living, welcome hope unto my heart,
help for my anguish sent, as it was destined,
oh celebrated day for me, long-sought.   4
    The hurt without relief which I deem blessèd
when, pained, I gave you life, I have forgot.
As if a sign to me that Heaven listened,
I was bestowed a rare gift, finely-wrought.   8
    Live, my belov'd, and with you may, I presage,
my own life live, and for your noble sire
his tired hope return to live in you.[41]   11
    If to be wise, strong, just you so desire,
you must rekindle, keep in mind as true
the splendor of your noble lineage.   14

---

[38]The large rooms of the castle of San Giustino were decorated with fresco paintings. See poem **18**.

[39]Poems **49–51**, which describe the author's motherly joys at the birth of her two sons, are the first of their kind in Italian poetry.

[40]As the author explicitly states in the printed text, this poem was written for her first son, Giulio, born in 1576.

[41]It must be remembered that Bufalini was eager for a male heir, since from his former marriages only daughters remained.

50.

Note the alternative rhyme in the *quartine*: ABAB/BABA.

Viscere del mio sen, cara pupilla
degli occhi miei, vezzoso pargoletto,
quanto di gioia il cor arde e sfavilla
qualor ti bacio e mi ti stringo al petto.   4
O con che dolce e che materno affetto
non madre pur, ma ti son fatta ancilla,
or ti vezzeggio or a dormir ti alletto
cantando e meno in ciò vita tranquilla.   8
Fra l'animate rose la mamella
talor ti porgo e il latte in un col core
ti dono e 'l prendi tu con gran diletto.   11
Mi ridi e miri e par che in tua favella
dica: "madre, gradisco un tanto amore,"
ma in vece del parlar, prendi l'affetto.   14

51.

Gioisci e canta, mio tranquillo core,
ch'il Ciel le giuste tue preghiere ha udito,
de la seconda prole t'ha arricchito,
e te pur teco il caro tuo signore.   4
Lungi i sospir, le lagrime 'l dolore:
l'inverno del penar è dipartito.
E godi seco d'un april fiorito
con dolce pace e sicurtà d'amore.   8
Felici notti, avventurosi giorni,
di godere il mio ben giunse pur l'ora,
ché vidi i desiati suoi ritorni.   11
E di frutti sì bei m'arricca ancora:
cresci, bambino e di splendor più s'orni
per te la patria e la prosapia onora.   14

50.

Dear focus of my eyes, fruit of my womb,
my charming little son, I must attest,
how full of joy my heart sparkles and burns
when I kiss you and press you to my breast.[42]	4
    As mother and maidservant, too, I turn
with such maternal feeling, oh, the sweetest,
now to caress you, and in dulcet tone
lull you to sleep; with tranquil life I'm blest.	8
    My nipple ringed with roses all in flower
I offer; with my milk, my heart as one
I give you, and you drink with greatest pleasure.	11
    You smile, regard me, seeming in your diction
to say: "Mother, so much love I do treasure,"
though you don't speak. Instead, you take affection.	14

51.[43]

Rejoice and sing, my heart, so reassured,
your righteous prayers have now been heard by Heaven
which has enriched you with a second son,
and placed with you again your dearest lord.[44]	4
    Away with sighs, with tears, with pain endured:
the winter of your grief is finally gone.
Enjoy with him April's full bloom, and one
with dulcet peace and with love most secured.	8
    Of happy nights and favorable days
of joy with my belov'd arrives the hour,
for his desired coming I foresaw.	11
    Rich fruits he bestows to me in all ways;
grow, my son, add to your country splendor
and to your noble lineage more honor.	14

---

[42]This sonnet, also written for Giulio and very different from the above (where the main joy was to have finally conceived an heir) vividly describes the joyous happiness of a young mother completely dedicated to her baby.

[43]This poem, as the author indicates, was written for the birth of her second son, Ottavio, born in 1582. No poems on her daughter, Camilla, born in 1579, are included in the printed edition of her *Rime*.

[44]This was another of her husband's returns from his duties in Rome.

LA MORTE DEL MARITO
(1583)

52.

Note that *ghiace* (line 2), is a poetic form for *giace*.

Ite, miei pianti, ove nascoso in terra
ghiace l'amato mio nobil tesoro,
il caro sposo, ond'io languisco e ploro,
ed è mia pace rivoltata in guerra.   4
Pur l'hai, Morte crudel, spento e sotterra?
Pur sarà sempiterno il mio martoro?
O tu Signor del sommo empireo coro
seco in quel marmo or or m'ascondi e serra.   8
Gelido marmo a cui s'invidia porto,
ché chiudi ogni mio ben perch'io non goda
lui, ch'era al viver mio pace e conforto.   11
O speranze sommerse entro nel porto!
O laccio che spezzato ancor m'annoda!
Dunque viver debb'io se egli è morto?   14

53.

Note the anaphora, or repeated emphatic use of *se* to introduce five sentences: *se goder — se concesso — se rimasa — se 'l cor — se cheggio* (lines 9–13), to conclude with the Baroque style, triple *morte* variants (lines 13–14).

Morte, se ben fatt'hai l'ultima possa
d'incenerir quella terrena scorza,
non fia però che per tuo inganno o forza,
la mia candida fè sia spenta o scossa.   4
Quell'ardor marital ch' andò per l'ossa
nel core, ond' arsi, il suo vigor rinforza,
né tempo il tempra o di questi occhi ammorza
onda di pianto nubilosa e grossa.   8

DEATH OF HER HUSBAND

The 24 poems, **52–75** of this section, written for the death of her husband (which occurred in 1583), were published in *Rime spirituali sopra i Misteri del Santissimo Rosario* (1595). They appear at the end of the book, pp. 149–72, under the subtitle, "In morte de l'illustrissimo signor Giulio Bufalini suo consorte." The original order has been maintained in our edition.

52.

Go forth, my cries, below the earth to where
lies hidden my belovèd noble treasure,
my spouse, while I remain, languish, implore,
with my peace now turned to internal war.   4
    Oh cruel Death, is he slain by you, interred?
Will I in torture be forevermore?
Oh Lord above, of the empyreal choir,
hide me within his marble vault, secured.   8
    Coldest marble, I desire your lot,
for you enclose my love, the one I sought
for peace in life, for comfort he inspired.   11
    Oh highest hopes submerged while reaching port!
Oh knot that, though unraveled, holds me taut!
If he is dead, is my life still required?   14

53.

Though clearly you have showed your might, oh Death,
your treachery or strength will never quell
or shake from my betrothed my candid faith
by making ashes of his[45] earthly shell.   4
    The wedding fire within my bones that dwelled
to light my heart, to burn, increases yet,
by time untempered; nor could waves that swell
from shedding, tearful eyes ever abate.   8

---

[45]Her husband's.

Ahi, se goder non l'ho potuto in vita,
se concesso mi fu per breve spazio,
se rimasa senz' alma e senza vita,   11
     se 'l cor del mondo fastidito è sazio,
se cheggio a Morte, incontro morte, aita,
Morte, pon fine a così lungo strazio.   14

54.

Note the Baroque use of antitheses in *pietà* [...] *spietata* (line 10) and in *fia luce* [...] *mancar del lume* (line 11). The poem concludes with *piangi, a pianger nata* (line 14), her leitmotif (see poems **1** and **21**).

     Morte crudel, tu sol, più dura assai
che pietra, a' preghi miei pur non ti muovi?
Almen m'uccidi e fia pietà ch'io provi
degli anni 'l fin, poi che non l'ho de' guai.   4
     Chiudimi gli occhi in sonno eterno e mai
non s'avivi mia speme o si rinnovi
il mio cipresso, e sol m'acqueti e giovi
pianto versar da lagrimosi rai,   8
     sol perch'io pera e mi distill' in fiume,
e fia pietà per me l'esser spietata,
e fia luce per me mancar del lume.   11
     Vedova, derelitta e sconsolata,
ahi, chi saldar tanto mio duol presume?
Anima, or sempre piangi, a pianger nata.   14

55.

     Ne l'atro abito mio si rappresenta
la mestizia ch'alberga entro nel core
che, vie più dentro che non mostra fuore,
lassa, m'ancide insidiosa e lenta.   4
     Né scema il grave duol che mi tormenta
per volger d'anni, anzi si fa maggiore,
ond' amo sol quel funeral colore
ch' il mio vedovo stato mi rammenta.   8

If fate deprives me of him in this world,
if he was with me for what seemed a moment,
if I am left bereft of life, of soul,   11
    if, sated, my bored heart should tire of earth,
if I ask Death to shore me against death,
oh Death, bring to an end such lengthy torment.   14

54.

Cruel Death, you only, harder than a stone,
are moved not by my prayers, though I beseech?
Kill me, at least, so my life's end I'll reach,
for pity's sake, and my torments atone.   4
    Let my hope rise not, nor my cypress stretch;
close both my eyes, and endless sleep condone,
and let me now find calmness here alone,
by shedding tears from eyes that weep and retch,   8
    so to a river I'll dissolve and die;
you'll show me pity, if you show no pity,
bestow me light, if you forgo my light.   11
    Oh, who'll resolve to heal this blow, for I
am widowed, derelict, disconsolate?
Cry out, my soul, you, born only to cry.[46]   14

55.

I see reflected here in my black dress
the sorrow that within my heart resides,
internal hurt which will not show outside,
insidious, slow, and killing me, alas!   4
    Nor does my great tormenting grief subside
as years go by; instead it just grows fuller,
so I love only this funereal color
which stamps the widowed state where I abide.   8

---

[46] Already used in poem **1**, also in the last line.

O dura impresa, o dolorosa insegna
de l'empia Morte, e sol de la mia vita
e del grado presagio afflitto e mesto.   11
     Ahi, chi mi fa d'ogni letizia indegna
ne l'età mia più verde e più fiorita?
Come il ben tardi viene e fugge presto!   14

56.

Se già per esser di sua luce priva,
restai senza 'l mio Sol fosca e piangente,
ché nulla poi rasserenò la mente:
d'altri e di me fastidiosa e schiva.   4
     Come spirar poss'io, com'esser viva?
Come mirar, come parlar sovente?
Parche, a lo stame mio perché pur lente?
Torcete il fil che l'alma abborre e schiva!   8
     Quanto, quanto è miglior tosto morire
per me, misera me, senza 'l mio bene,
che viver sol, per sempre mai languire.   11
     O mia forte aventura, o pianti, o pene!
Ben d'ogni altro più duro è quel martire
ch' ammorza e secca in sul fiorir la spene.   14

57.

Here Turini Bufalini uses a Baroque conceit in claiming that her *sospiri* acquire *sete* in the *umore,* liquid of her tears, that burns and consumes her (lines 6–8). The result is an antithesis: she is nourished by her tears, and instead of *morte,* receives *vita* (lines 10–11).

O miei vedovi, tristi, oscuri lumi,
meravigliom'io ben s'ancor vedete,
se la notte, se 'l dì, sempre piangete,
occhi non già, ma due correnti fiumi.   4
     Mai non cangiate voi stili o costumi,
sempre pianti e sospir del cor traete,
sospir che ne l'umore acquistan sete,
umore ond'io me n'arda e mi consumi.   8

Oh stark impression, painful outward sign
of wicked Death; you bleak augur of mine,
telling my life's affliction, my unease.   11
  Who marks me undeserving, to resign
my joy, my verdant bloom to undermine?
How happiness comes late; how fast it flees! 14

56.

In darkness do I go without his light,
without my Sun, in tears, and desolate,
for nothing calms my mind in such a state:
a bore no one at all would tolerate.   4
  How can I breathe, how live now, in this plight?
How can I speak, how do my eyes have sight?
Oh Fates[47] who wind my thread, why hesitate?
Cut off the thread my soul abhors and hates! 8
  How much, much brighter would it be, alas,
bereft of love, to die within the hour,
than live only to languish evermore.   11
  Oh hapless luck, oh tears, how will this pass!
The greatest pain is one that with such power
can sap and suck hope dry in its first flower. 14

57.

Oh widowed eyes of mine, sad and obscure,
how you can still see light I cannot say,
since crying is your course by night, by day,
two running rivers, but two eyes no more. 4
  And this one style of yours you don't betray,
but draw from out my heart tears and sighs ever;
sighs, which gain thirst in this liquid humor,
liquid where, consumed, I burn away.   8

---

[47]Fates, or Parcae, the three goddesses who presided over the birth and life of mankind.
Clotho spun the thread of life, Lachesis determined its length and Atropos cut it.

Per maggior pena, o dispietata sorte,
tra due contrari in perigliosa guerra,
vita ricevo, onde devria la morte.   11
    O sfortunata sovr' ogni altra in terra,
poi ch' umana pietà chiuso ha le porte,
quelle, tu Re del Ciel, m'apri e disserra.   14

58.

Vonne = *me ne vo*; *ghiace* = poetic for *giace* (line 3); *vuo'* = *voglio* (line 8).

Spinta talora d'ardente desio,
con gli occhi al cielo e 'l cor tutto rivolto,
vonne ove ghiace il mio signor sepolto,
tra l'ombra del silenzio e de l'oblio.   4
    Quivi, resi gli onor debiti a Dio,
mi stringo e struggo e di nove onde il volto
spargo e sospiro. Ahi, pensier vano e stolto,
se quel vuo' che non puote esser più mio!   8
    Con la voce del cor prego e richiamo,
e dico lui: deh, sarà mai quel giorno,
ch'io ponga fine al duolo ed a la vita?   11
    Sarà ch'io torni a quel, che cotant' amo,
sciolta dal corpo, ove han pace e soggiorno
quei che son scritti al libro de la vita?   14

59.

Note the alternative rhyme in the *quartine*: ABAB/BABA.

Volgi gli occhi dal Ciel, dolce e pietoso
Signor, verso i miei figli orfani a cui
togliesti il padre, il mio diletto sposo,
sì disponendo i gran giudizi tui.   4
    Ch'a te ricorso abbiam, non ad altrui,
in sì lugubre stato e lagrimoso.
Mira come da te, dolenti e bui,
non altronde attendiam pace e riposo.   8

Pitiless fate, you deal me greater hurt,
for, torn between two foes in warring strife,
I'd prefer death; instead, I'm given life.   11
    Oh wretched woman, I, from all on earth,
since human pity turns me from its doors,
You, King of Heaven, unlock, open Yours.   14

58.

    At times when fiery longing spurs me forward,
with eyes and heart to Heaven do I turn,
midst shades of silence and oblivion,   4
to seek that place where buried lies my lord.
    And having paid the tribute due to God,
I bathe my face with tears, I break and burn
in waves and sighs. Oh, useless thought, to yearn
for something that can never be restored!   8
    With my heart's voice I call out and I pray
declaring: — will there ever be a day
when I will see the end of life and grief?   11
    Will it be soon when I'll rejoin my love,
from body free, and peaceful sojourn have,
as those inscribed within the book of life?   14

59.

    From Heaven turn Your eyes, compassionate,
sweet Lord, as in Your judgment great You chose
to take from my two sons, orphaned of late,
their father, my most dear, belovèd spouse.   4
    On no one but You can we now impose,
in our abject and pitiable state.
Look how, from You alone, peace and repose
we must, sorrowed and suffering, await.   8

Deh, rimira, Signor, lunge e d'intorno:
più d'un leon che con aperte brame
volgon contro di noi l'ugne e 'l rugito.   11
    Oh, sarà dunque mai, sarà quel giorno,
ch'alme sovenga dolorose e grame
e plachi 'l mar e ne riduca al lito?   14

60.

Fortuna e Morte unite a' nostri danni,
l'estremo, o figli, fan d'ogni potere,
senza pietà, senza risguardo avere
ai miei lugubri, ai vostri tener' anni.   4
    Qual gregge inerme ove crudel l'azzanni
morso d'inique e dispietate fere,
quasi 'n selva d'orrori ove io despere
armi al contrasto o per la fuga i vanni.   8
    Sol ne resta virtù, conforto e speme
ne la benignità di quel Signore,
che placa il mar quando più irato freme,   11
    forse rimetterà nel suo bel fiore
l'illustre casa e goderemo insieme
gli ozi e la pace d'un concorde amore.   14

61.

Del mio vedovo cor, speme e conforto,
dolci miei pargoletti, amati e cari,
sarà già mai che d'esti flutti amari,
con voi mi tragga a salvamento in porto?   4
    Ahi, quanti affanni e sol per voi sopporto!
Quante, contro Fortuna, armi e ripari
trovar convienmi a rintuzzar gli avari
colpi suoi, ver noi crudi a sì gran torto!   8
    Né di Socrate aver la pazienza,
né di quei sette, onde la Grecia ha vanto:
arte, senno, valor, forza e prudenza,   11

Oh Lord, look all around us far and near:
more than one lion[48] here, agape with greed,
show up to threaten us with claws and roars.   11
    Oh, will it be, will ever day appear,
to offer help to our souls, so in need,
to calm the sea and lead us to safe shores?   14

60.

    Despite my widowed state, your age so tender,
in harming us, Fortune and Death unite
and do their utmost, children,[49] with their might,
to show no mercy, no regard confer.   4
    But like a helpless herd, seized by the bite
of wild, cruel, evil beasts in massacre,
I cannot hope, within this glade of horror,
for arms to fight, or any wings for flight.   8
    Our virtue is our comfort; our reward
lies with the divine goodness of that Lord
who calms the sea at height of stormy rage.   11
    Would that to its first splendor be restored
our house illustrious, that He assuage
our grief with peace, repose and love's accord.   14

61.

    Sweet children, my belovèd little ones,
hope of my widowed heart, and only comfort,
will it be, through rough waves and jettisons
I'll anchor with you safe someday in port?   4
    Such grief I'll ford, and for you I'll support!
How many arms, how many garrisons
against Fortune must I find, her strikes to thwart,
her blows so cruel to us, unjustly done!   8
    For I have none of Socrates' patience,
nor virtues seven that Greece holds so dear:
art, wisdom, valor, strength or even prudence,   11

---

[48]Metaphor for the enemies of the author and her children.
[49]The author addresses her own children.

né gridar giova o lagrimar in tanto,
ché Fortuna, spogliando ogni clemenza,
pur vuol ch'io pera e mi distill' in pianto.　　　14

62.

O vago e bel giardin, ove già spesso
col vivo Sol de la speranza mia,
or nel prato, or nel bosco ombroso e spesso,
per verde andava e spaziosa via.　　　4
　　Chi tanto ben m'invola? Ah, perché adesso
non godo in te quel che goder solìa?
Il pianto e 'l sospirar sol m'è concesso
senza l'amata e dolce compagnia.　　　8
　　L'erbe, le piante, i fior, gli arbori e i sassi
veggion l'umor, che da quest'occhi innonda,
e i pensier duri e i dolorosi passi.　　　11
　　Ma pur non ho chi per pietà risponda
a' miei concenti, lagrimosi e lassi,
o tempri 'l duol, che dal mio petto abonda.　　　14

63.

See comments to poem **27** for the enumeration of the various elements of nature.

O vago e dilettevole boschetto,
poggio di linfe e di bei fiori adorno,
ove sovente a trapassar del giorno
vengo le noie e 'l amoroso affetto.　　　4
　　Mentre in voi stommi, ahi, che l'usato obbietto
pur mi si para a la memoria intorno,
né le dolci aure, o può sì bel soggiorno,
lassa, un leve sospir tormi dal petto.　　　8
　　Non tante han quei cipressi o questi abeti
frondi, né stille il fonte o l'mare arene,
né tante il cielo stelle o fiori il prato,　　　11
　　quant' i miei dì, che fur sereni e lieti,
e quanti gli occhi miei fuor d'ogni usato
(spento il vivo mio Sol) tormenti e pene.　　　14

nor does it good to cry, to call laments,
for Fortune, who casts off all clemency,
would have me die, distilled into a tear.   14

62.

Oh lovely, beautiful garden where I could,
so often with the bright Sun of my hope,
in meadows and in dense and shady wood,
go stroll on many a green and spacious slope.   4
    Who did with all my happiness elope?
Why do I not find joy here, as I should?
With only tears and sighs now must I cope
without my sweet beloved, in widowhood.   8
    The grass, the plants, the flowers and trees, the rock
can see the liquid[50] flowing from my eyes,
my hardened thoughts, my sorrow-laden walk.   11
    Yet no one will in pity empathize,
give answer to my plaintive, weary talk,
or temper pain when my heart-floods arise.   14

63.

Oh little forest, fair, full of delight,
and knoll that water and bright flowers adorn,
where frequently I come to disunite
myself from daily care and love forlorn;   4
    within me once again his face well-known,
alas, even here, memory brings in sight,
nor can this dulcet air, this place of charm
more weight take from my sighs, make my heart light.   8
    No twigs count more in cypress or in fir,
nor does the spring have drops, nor sea more sand,
nor meadow blooms, nor sky as many stars   11
    as have my days, once gay, free of despair,
and my two eyes, torments beyond compare,
since, spent, my living Sun went from this land.   14

---

[50]Tears.

64.

Ben so ragionar io come per arte
de le nott' infelici e tristi giorni,
degl'inganni di Morte e degli scorni,
ma non ho stil che ben lo spieghi in carte.   4
    Né cercar valmi or questa or quella parte,
non vaghe fonti o bei giardini adorni,
ché quei non fan che la smarrita torni
allegrezza del cor, quando si parte.   8
    Lassa, non scema, no, piccol gioire,
saldo pensier d' un'amorosa brama,
anzi cresce nel ben spesso il martire.   11
    Tal io, spento il mio Sol, misera e grama,
se mai cerco rimedio al mio languire,
tanto il cor più si duol, quanto più l'ama.   14

65.

The theme of *sonno* [sleep] was treated by several poets of the Cinque and Seicento, including Giovanni della Casa, in his famous *O sonno, o de la queta, umida, ombrosa / notte placido figlio.... oblio dolce de' mali* (Ferroni, p. 127, XVII, lines 1–3). But instead of calling sleep *figlio de la notte,* Turini Bufalini uses *fratel de la vita* (line 5).

Tranquillo oblio, che negli amplessi tuoi
(mentre ne tien) dai nutrimento e vita;
sonno, l'aura di cui da me sparita,
nulla ho senso o pensier che non m'annoi.   4
    O fratel de la vita, or se non vuoi
ch'io langua e pera in tanto male, aita
porgi a l'anima afflitta e sbigottita,
che te sol chere, e consolar la puoi.   8
    Torna già dolce, or sospirato sonno,
e gustar fammi entr' il ruscel di Lete,
un sorso tal che se n'appaghi 'l core.   11
    Tu vedi ben che gli occhi miei non ponno
chiudersi unquanco o ritrovar quiete,
e ch'io son presso al terminar de l'ore.   14

64.

I know well how to artfully expound
on many an unhappy night and morn,
on Death's deceit and no less on her scorn,
but I have not the style to write it down.   4
    Nor is it any use to look around
for lovely springs or gardens well-adorned;
those things will not bring me lost joy's return
to fill my heart again, now joy is gone.   8
    Alas, a simple joy cannot undo
a solid thought of longing for amour;   11
the more my joy, the more my pain does grow.
    Without my Sun, and wretched and heartsore,
if ever I seek joy to cure my woe,
the more I hurt, the more I love him so.   14

65.

Oblivion,[51] within your tranquil arms,
(while you hold tight) you give me food and life.
And Sleep, since you departed with your charms,
no feeling have I that does not bring strife.   4
    Brother of life, if you don't wish me harm
to suffer so and perish in such grief,
please help my soul, afflicted and disarmed,
which yearns only for you and your relief.   8
    Return again as sweet and longed-for sleep.
Let me of Lethe's[52] waters drink so deep,
and taste a drop to satiate my heart.   11
    You see quite well that my two eyes can weep,
but cannot close at all, nor will rest keep;
the ending of my days draws near its start.   14

---

[51]Oblivion found in sleep, a frequent subject in Italian Renaissance poetry.
[52]Lethe, the river from which the souls of the dead drank, before entering Hades, in order to achieve oblivion from their memory of life.

66.

O miseri occhi miei, se mai chiudete
per stanchezza le luci, afflitti e vinti,
com'è ch'al vostro mal tosto correte,
per istrani 'ntricati laberinti?   4
    Come esser puote in voi pace o quiete,
d'ombre, di larve e di follie dipinti
sogni, o sogni crudei, che m'accrescete
vero duol in piacer fugaci e finti?   8
    Ché talor mi mostrate il signor mio,
con faccia sì serena e sì gioconda,
che mi sembra il vegghiar saldo e verace.   11
    Ma mentre in tal dolcezza il core abonda,
voi, ritornando nel cimmerio oblio,
me lasciate di lui priva e di pace.   14

67.

    S'a lo specchio talor stringo o raccolgo
il crin negletto e i negri orridi veli,
par che tutt' il mio duol s'apra e riveli,
mentre i bianchi capei tra i biondi avolgo.   4
    A me stessa allor penso e mi rivolgo
perché sempre io più pianga e mi quereli,
e dico: ah, ben si van cangiando i peli,
gli affanni no, che tutt' in me raccolgo;   8
    questi son pure ingiusti agli anni miei,
ché per mio mal non sono ancor sì innante
ch'esser debban di neve in verd' etade.   11
    O Fortuna crudele, iniqui e rei
travagli, ond'io fra tante pene e tante
trovo aperte al mio mal tutte le strade.   14

66.

Oh miserable, saddened eyes of mine,
if, vanquished by fatigue, your lights do wane,
why must you run so quickly to entwine
yourselves in labyrinths[53] of tangled pain?   4
    Peace and repose in you how can I find
among your shades and specters, dreams insane;
oh cruel dreams, why do you deceive my mind
and increase hurt with joy that won't remain?   8
    For now and then my lord[54] you show to me
with countenance so cheerful and serene
that the illusion seems reality.   11
    But as my heart abounds in that sweet scene,
you leave me for your dark oblivion,
deprived of him and of tranquillity.   14

67.

    If, at the mirror, gathering in my hands
my frightful veil of black, my unkempt hair,
it seems my pain appears to me, laid bare,
as I braid in the white with the blonde strands.   4
    I ask myself why I cry unrestrained,
and say: — I see the changes in my hair,
in my woes, no, all gathered in me there.   8
And these, my woes, grow ever more abundant,
    and to my years are unjustly allied.
Alas, though not yet old, I've come to know,
in greenest years, hair turned as white as snow.   11
    Oh Fortune cruel, and travails you bestow,
why do I, midst your torments multiplied,
find every way to my hurt open wide?   14

---

[53]Intricate dreams.
[54]Her husband.

68.

Note the alternative rhyme in the *quartine*: ABBA/BAAB.

Misera vita mia! Qual fui? Qual sono?
Già solea esercitar musico canto,
vaghe carole, altere rime e quanto
può tasto o plettro armonioso e buono.   4
Or la citara mia rivolta in pianto,
sol cordoglio e sospir da l'alma intono.
Odon le selve il lagrimabil suono:
Eco risponde e se ne porta il vanto   8
pur da quel primo dì ch'orrida vesta
e negra benda a l'affannata vita
cinsi, d'oscurità sparsa e contesta.   11
Né può l'anima, afflitta e sbigottita,
moto o voce formar che non sia mesta,
o rima che non sia frale e smarrita.   14

69.

O miei sciocchi pensier, voi pur mirate
sempre in quel che m'arreca ira e tormento!
Io pur, colpa di voi, ravolgo e sento
presente 'l mal de le miserie andate.   4
Perché sempre languir, voglie ostinate?
Ché se ne volan gli anni 'n un momento,
ed è leve il dolor come il contento
e più d'un vetro fral: quanto sperate?   8
Se bramate gioir, convienvi al Cielo
da terra alzar con velocissim' ale.
Ivi è gioia, piacer, pace e quiete.   11
Ivi, accese di puro ardente zelo,
vedrete quanto sia fugace e frale
quel ben ch' invan qua giù tanto piangete.   14

68.

My wretched life! Who was I once? And now?
Musical song did I once exercise
and, as I could, in key harmonious,
high rhyme pluck out and ballads strong and true.   4
    Now does my cithara turn lachrymose,
and my soul intones only sighs and sorrow.
The forests hear the tearful tremolo:
and back to me Echo responds to boast   8
    of that first day in which a dress so horrid
I donned, and the black band to my life tied,
a life entwined with darkness, strewn, oppressed.   11
    No longer can my soul, wounded, afraid,
form word or syllable that's not distressed,
or rhyme that is not feeble and so lost.   14

69.

My foolish thoughts, why must you always dwell
on things that only raise my rage and torment!
It's fault of yours that I feel ever-present
the pain of my past miseries in this vale.   4
    And stubborn longings, why must you prevail?
As given, years fly by in just an instant,
and sorrow is but brief, brief as contentment.
How much hope can you draw from glass so frail?   8
    If joy you covet, to Heaven appeal
to lift you up from earth on wings most agile.
There do joy, pleasure, peace and quiet keep.   11
    There, burning with a pure and ardent zeal
will you then see how fleeting and how fragile
the want that in vain down here you so weep.   14

70.

Paolo Bà prefers to read line 7 as: *che d'amor fugacissmo, e ribella.*

Misera, io voglio accompagnar mia sorte
con quella sconsolata tortorella,
che priva piange, in questa parte e in quella,
del suo fedel l'intempestiva morte.   4
Sì la punge dolor tenace e forte,
sì del suo danno geme e si rappella
che d'amor fugacissimo è ribella,
scompagnata se n' va senza consorte.   8
Tal io, misera me! Senza aver speme
nel mondo, albergo d'ira e di dolore,
il resto viver vuo' de la mia vita.   11
Con lei solinga rimarromm' insieme
senza novo provar secondo amore
infin al dì de l'ultima partita.   14

71.

Queste lagrime amare in copia tante
che versar gli occhi miei con tal dolore,
questi che traggi alti sospir dal core
ché non li volgi al primo eterno Amante?   4
Anima sconsolata! A lui davante
manda le strida ad ammendar l'errore;
spegni le fiamme de l'antico ardore,
troppo ormai fiere al sentimento errante.   8
Per le cose qua giù t'affliggi e duoli
mai sempre, ingrata, e sofferir ti spiace
danni, doni di Dio graditi e cari.   11
Deh, perché il Cielo a te medesma involi?
Perché non porti 'l tormentare in pace
e, languendo, a gioir ché non impari?   14

70.

In misery, I would my fate compare
to that young, tender dove, disconsolate,
deprived, who weeps now over here, now there,
her faithful consort's death, untimely met.   4
    Oh, how it stings her, pain so hard to bear.
Oh, how she coos her loss, so to berate,
rebel, at love that too soon disappears,
and uncompanioned goes without her mate.   8
    Thus I, in misery, no hope to have
on this earth, host to anger and to pain,
with no hope will the rest of life live out,   11
    and solitary with her I'll remain
and will not try a new and second love
until the day my parting's ultimate.   14

71.

These tears so bitter and too much abundant
which from my eyes with so much pain are drawn,
along with those deep sighs from my heart rent,
why not to the eternal, first Love turn,   4
    oh, soul disconsolate! Before Him prone,
send forth your cries that error you'd repent,
and douse the flames of old with which you burn,
grown too fierce now with errant sentiment.   8
    For earthly things you pine eternal, yearn,
while, ungrateful, to suffer you despise
life's damages, dear gifts of God most gracious.   11
    Tell me, why is it Heaven from you flies?
Why don't you bear your sadness here in peace
and to be glad, in decline, won't you learn?   14

72.

Quando torno in me stessa e penso, ahi lassa,
quant' offeso ha Gesù l'anima mia,
sento pena nel cor sì cruda e ria,
che, quasi acuto stral, l'ancide e passa.   4
    E dico: ahi meschinella, ignuda e cassa
d'ingegno e fuor de la diritta via,
s'ombra di morte è quel ch'uom più desia
che vuoi da speme sì terrena e bassa?   8
    Misera, inutilmente lagrimando
spendi 'l tuo tempo e pace unqua non hai,
né pensi al disbrigarti 'l come o 'l quando.   11
    Volgi, deh, volgi al Ciel gli umidi rai,
il mondo fuggi e pon gli affetti 'n bando,
ché del quinci partir l'ora non sai.   14

73.

Ché prendi, anima mia, cotanto affanno,
de le cure del mondo egre e noiose?
Volgi, deh, volgi al Ciel le rugiadose
luci al Rettor de l'alto empireo scanno.   4
    Né membrar l'altrui torto o 'l proprio danno
tra queste vane e transitorie cose,
ché quel nocchier ch'in alto mar ti pose
schiveratti di quell'ira e inganno.   8
    Ecco, se pur sovente invide, avare
onde t'han scorto e tu se' viva ancora,
è salva, sua mercè, tua fragil nave.   11
    Deh, cessa il pianto e l'aspre pene amare,
dura, alma, spera, e 'n fin a l'ultim' ora
soffri e per Dio soffrir non ti sia grave.   14

72.

When, coming to my senses, I inquire
how much my soul deserves Jesus' wrath,
a piercing pain I feel within my heart,
so arrow-like that I nearly expire.   4
    I say then: — wretched one, bereft of thought,
when souls of men Death's shadow most desire,
why to such base and earthly hope aspire?
You surely now have strayed from the true path.   8
    Downcast one, time spent crying is a loss,
as your peace you have nowhere come across,
nor do you know how, when you'll disengage.   11
    To Heaven turn, oh turn your weeping visage,
flee from the world, your passion from you toss;
the striking of your hour you cannot presage.   14

73.

My soul, why anguish so, why agonize
with tedious, unhealthy, worldly care;
to Heaven turn, oh turn your teary eyes
unto the Ruler of the highest sphere.   4
    Forget your loss, and your past injuries,
and all this hollow, transitory fare,
or boatman[55] who must row you to high seas,
will shun you for your anger and despair.   8
    If waves of envy tossed you in their wake —
miserly waves — you live, have breathing space;
safe is your fragile boat, willed by His grace.   11
    Oh, weep no more, from bitter torment break;
endure, hope, till death suffering embrace,
and suffering bear, no burden for God's sake.   14

---

[55]Who transports the souls of the dead.

74.

The *breve viver che m'avanza* (line 6), recalls Petrarch's *il viver breve che n'avanza* (*Rime*, CLXVIII, line 14).

Benedetto sia 'l dì che gli occhi alzai
al primo Amor de l'alta empirea stanza;
quest' è tutto il mio ben, la mia speranza,
del cor oggetto e de' piangenti rai.   4
    Dolci mi son per lui le pene e i guai,
di questo breve viver che m'avanza,
e dolce, fuor d'ogni mortale usanza,
morirne al fin, s'io l'otterrò già mai.   8
    Ben mia sorte felice dir poss' io,
se cieca vissi già tanti e tanti anni,
or m'apre gli occhi il mio Signore e Dio,   11
    che, perché io scerna i sempiterni danni,
spesso mi dice, mansueto e pio:
"Deh, fuggi 'l mondo e i suoi proterv' inganni."   14

75.

In this madrigal, Turini Bufalini praises the poetic style of Vittoria Colonna, who wrote with *dotte, angeliche, parole, / con rime alte e famose* (lines 6–7), and adorned the sky with her *bel Sole* (line 8), while Francesca's style is only *semplice e frale* (line 10). It should be kept in mind that the author alludes to the concluding *terzina* of Colonna's introductory sonnet *Amaro lacrimar, non dolce canto, / foschi sospiri e non voce serena / di stil no ma di duol mi danno vanto* (*Rime*, I, lines 12–14).

Porti Vittoria il vanto
di stil, non di dolore,
ché de la vena onde si strugge il core
l'arte ho minor, ma non minor il pianto.   4
Tu chiamasti Parnaso, ei ti rispose,
al suon di dotte, angeliche parole,
con rime alte e famose,
adornandone il ciel del tuo bel Sole.   8

74.

To the first Love of the empyreal sphere,
blest be the day I lifted up my gaze.
He is my only love, my hope always,
the object of my heart, my eyes, my tears.   4
    For Him, sweet are the troubles and the fear
of this short life and my remaining stay;
and sweet again, past any mortal way
will be my death, if ever death draw near.   8
    And surely happy is my destiny,
if for so many years I had no sight,
since my Lord God opened my eyes for me.   11
    And so to save me from eternal night,
He tells me often, gently, piously:
"Flee from the world, its arrogant deceit."   14

75.[56]

You shall the glory, Vittoria,[57] be keeping
for higher style, but not, I think, for sorrow;
for of that vein which rends, destroys my heart now,
I have less art, not less pain, or less weeping.   4
You[58] called upon Parnassus,[59] which responded
to learnèd words and to angelic sound,
with sublime verse and with your rhyme renowned,
and thus the sky your brilliant Sun[60] adorned.   8

---

[56]This concluding poem is a madrigal, the only one in the series.

[57]Vittoria Colonna, in whose verses Francesca recognizes a superior poetic style, but not a greater grief. This competition reveals Turini Bufalini's desire to achieve recognition as a poet.

[58]Vittoria.

[59]Parnassus, a mountain of Phocis (Greece), consecrated to the Muses and Apollo.

[60]"Sun," metaphor used by Colonna for her husband. It was also used by Francesca and reappears as such in line 13 of this madrigal, which concludes the series of poems on the death of Giulio Bufalini in the 1595 edition of *Rime sacre*.

Misera, io piango e male
Pindo ascolta il mio dir semplice e frale,
ch'io crederei s'eguale
fosse 'l mio stile a la pietade e al zelo,
ornar anch'io d'un novo sole il cielo.   13

But for my part, in pain I cry, alas,
my weak, plain style not heard too well by Pindus;[61]
if style, though, equaled zeal or feelings pious,
if style for tears were given one for one,
I, too, would gild the sky with a new Sun.   13

---

[61]Pindus, a chain of mountains between Thessaly and Macedonia, consecrated to the Muses and Apollo, while Parnassus was its most famous peak.

La lunga vedovanza: lamenti, difficoltà, figli e nipoti, ricordi e vecchiaia

76.

Brevi allegrezze de l'umana vita
che, qual foco di paglia, trapassate,
e qual leve balen vi dileguate,
ahi, ch'ogni gioia s'è da me partita. 4
 Il mio cor, la mia speme e la mia vita
Morte mi ha tolto, e in tenebre ecclissate
le luci mie, che ne le luci amate
mirava, ond' al mio mal non spero aita. 8
 Che farò, lassa, in così duro stato
senza 'l mio Sol, sort' empia? Ahi, rio destino
che l'hai sul fior del mio gioir levato. 11
 Fa ch'io prenda ver lui tosto il camino,
che se m'hai tolto il mio tesor da lato
possa sepolta almen stargli vicino. 14

77.

Era a te poco, ahi cruda, avermi tolto
appena io nata, il mio gran genitore,
per cui peregrinai del nido fuore
lunga stagion, con lacrimoso volto. 4
 Se a maggior danni il tuo pensier rivolto
per farmi piaga sempiterna al core,
non sentia per la madre il tuo furore,
Morte, ond' hai seco ogni mio ben sepolto. 8

A Long Widowhood: Laments, Difficulties, Children and Grandchildren, Remembrances and Old Age

The poems in this section, **76–139**, are from *Rime,* pp. 166–310 (a selection), while the last two, **140–41**, are from Vittorio Corbucci's book on Turini Bufalini.

76.

Brief joys of human life that hold our trust,
like flames of kindled straw, you burn to ash,
you vanish, much like lightning in a flash;
ah, thus for me, all joy has turned to dust.   4
  Death all my hope, my heart, my life has slashed;
my eyes, eclipsed, in darkness has she thrust,
my life, beheld in eyes belovèd most,
so any hope to quell my pain is dashed.   8
  What shall I do in such a bitter state
without my Sun, cruel Fortune? Oh, cruel fate
who plucked him when my joy was just in bloom.   11
  Show me the path to him, let me not wait,
since from my side you stole my treasured mate,
entomb me, that I may lie next to him.   14

77.

Not quite enough, oh cruel one, to be robbing
my noble father from me at my birth,
and far from home, force me to wander, sobbing,
through many a season, everywhere on earth;   4
  but greater damage at me you'd be lobbing
to strike eternal wound upon my heart,
as Mother stood against your fury's probing,
you buried all my good with her, oh Death.   8

Né sazia, ingorda, il caro mio consorte
mi rapisti, e le gioie al mio diletto
hai nel mar del mio pianto amaro absorte.   11
     Or se lugubre è 'l crin, vedovo il letto,
tronca le fila del mio stame attorto,
ch'ond' ebbi io piaga, or medicina aspetto.   14

78.

O per me giorno memorabil tanto,
giorno duro per me, giorno infelice,
che svellesti il mio cor da la radice,
onde sparso ho dagli occhi un mar di pianto.   4
     Tu mi togliesti 'l mio tesor da canto,
per cui giva sì altera e sì felice,
ed ora solo il lagrimar mi lice
e vedova mi lagno in negro manto.   8
     Quanto, lassa, perdei, quanto Fortuna
m'ha percosso e m'è ognor più cruda e fera,
senza pietade aver da parte alcuna.   11
     L'alma misera mia, s'ange e dispera,
ché a penar cominciò fin da la cuna,
per tua pietà, Dio, non voler ch'io pera.   14

79.

Dopo un lungo vegghiar là su l'aurora,
ai sensi immersi nel liquor di Lete,
il sonno entrò per vie tacite e quete,
ch'esser pareami d'ogni noia fuora.   4
     Dentro un vago giardin, pompa di Flora,
vidi venir, con luci amiche e liete,
il mio sposo, e con note alme e discrete
dirmi, porgendo la sua destra ancora: 8
     "Perché del mio partir t'affliggi e lagni?
Se sapessi quel ben ch'io provo in Cielo,
gioiresti per quel ch'in darno piagni.   11

Voracious, you have now snatched, never sated,
my husband dear; the joys of my delight
in my sea of sour tears you have absorbed.   11
    My hair lugubrious, widowed my bed,
sever the strings of my life's twisted thread,
for I, wounded, your medicine await.[62]   14

78.

I'll not forget you, indelible day,[63]
my heart its very root eradicated
by sad and unendurable dismay,
my eyes their sea of tears begun to shed.   4
    For from my side, my prize you plucked away,
with whom I was so gay, of whom so proud;
with only crying left me to convey,
a widow, I lament, in my black shroud.   8
    Alas, how much I lost; how badly Fortune
did batter me with blows so fierce and cruel,
without a shred of care from anyone.   11
    And hope abandons my despairing soul
whose suffering was born within its cradle.
Let me not perish, Lord, by pity shunned.   14

79.

At dawn, after a sleepless night I lay,[64]
quiet came sleep upon me, peacefully,
my senses steeped in the liquor of Lethe;
I felt as though all care had crept away.   4
    Within a garden fair, Flora's[65] display,
I saw come forth, with gay eyes, happily,
my spouse, with words discrete, well-known to me,
his right hand proffering; I heard him say: 8
    "Why do you grieve my death? Why do you plea?
If my heavenly life you could but see,
you would rejoice and not uselessly wail.   11

---

[62]The author creates an interesting conceit, perceiving death as a medicine that will heal the wounds of life.

[63]The day her husband died.

[64]The theme of the poem is derived from Petrarch, who saw Laura in a dream and was told by her that she is waiting for him in heaven.

[65]Flora, the goddess of flowers and gardens.

Qual ti promisi con pietade e zelo,
invoco Dio ché sempre t'accompagni,
fin che sciolta sarai del mortal velo."   14

80.

Stanca dal pianto, presso al dì dormendo,
sovragiunger mi parve il mio bel Sole,
di cui priva 'l mio cor s'affligge e duole,
e sembravami star meco sedendo.   4
    Egli lieta la faccia a me volgendo
diceami con dolcissime parole:
"Ahi, perché non voler quel che 'l Ciel vuole?
Perché, misera, stai sempre piangendo?   8
    Fin da l'Empireo i lagrimosi umori
veggio, ed odo i sospiri; ch'io mai diviso
non son da te, deh, tempra i tuoi dolori."   11
    Ma con pietosa man, mentre ch'il viso
m'asciuga, fugge 'l sogno, e i dolci errori
scorgo e di doglia il cor resta conquiso.   14

81.

Caro mio ben, quel tuo verace amore,
che in mille modi ognor m'hai dimostrato,
il largo e nobil don che m'hai lasciato
più manifesta, e 'l liberal tuo core.   4
    Ché fin che del mio fin non giungan l'ore
vuoi ch'io splendida viva al modo usato,
e che delle tue regge a me sia dato
l'uso, ond'io serbi il solito splendore.   8
    E quinci non potrà tempo né loco
far che la tua pietà ponga in oblio
e che non arda del tuo nobil foco.   11
    Sempre sta in te rivolto il pensier mio,
e sempre te la notte e 'l giorno invoco,
e dove stai venir chieggio e desio.   14

As I have promised you with love and zeal,
I pray God that He will your escort be,
until the day you're free of mortal veil.[66]   14

80.

Tired out by tears, I slept at break of dawn,
when suddenly seated just at my side
it seemed to me I saw my lovely Sun
without whom my heart does in grief abide.   4
    With happy face to me he seemed to turn,
to tell me with sweet words so dignified:
"Oh, why do you not wish what's wished by Heaven?
Your tears and cries will you not put aside?   8
    From Heaven, I perceive your tearful humor[67]
and hear your sighs; since I'm not separate
from you, your pain, oh, do please moderate."   11
    My face he dries with hand compassionate,
whence the dream flees, and its bittersweet error
I realize; again he leaves me heartsore.[68]   14

81.

The noble gift[69] you left to me, belovèd,
displays your great and open-handed heart,
and that true love of yours you did impart,
which in a thousand ways to me you proved.   4
    For up to my last hour, whence I'll depart,
in splendor you have willed that I shall live,
that all your palaces may be preserved
and used in all their splendor with their art.   8
    No place, nor any time that may transpire,
could cause me to forget that loving stroke,
and never will they quench my passion's fire.   11
    My thoughts are with you always, whole, entire,
as night and day I call you, and invoke,
where you are I would go, and so desire.   14

[66]Metaphor for body, used by Petrarch.
[67]Tears.
[68]See note 64 to poem **79**.
[69]Giulio Bufalini's last will, favoring Francesca (see Introduction.)

82.

O mio tetto real, loco divino,
mar per me di dolcezze, or di dolore,
mentre godei l'amato mio signore —
gioia, or pena qual vuole empio destino.   4
    O florido, o giocondo mio giardino,
ove andai con mio ben spendendo l'ore;
or piango, ed al mio pianto, al mio clamore,
da speco mi risponde Eco vicino.   8
    O stanze già sì ornate, ricche sale,
or piene sol di paventosi orrori,
in cui languisco d'insanabil male.   11
    Quando mai fine avran gli aspri dolori?
Tempo e loco cangiar nulla mi vale,
ché i miei lutti si fan sempre maggiori.   14

83.

Tiferno mio, stanza mia dolce e cara,
ove la bella età lieta varcai;
breve è stato il gioir, ma lunghi i guai,
poiché spense il mio Sol, notte atra, amara.   4
    Vissi in te seco, or un' breve urna avara
chiude seco il mio cor, né spero mai
pace, o pur tregua, a' miei penosi lai,
e, languendo, il morir l'anima impara.   8
    Sol la torbida mente e 'l tardo ingegno
soccorse Apollo, a la cui dolce aita
di Fortuna crudel temprai lo sdegno.   11
    E s'averrà ch' a l'ultima partita
sien mie reliquie unite al dolce pegno,
dirò che, morta, entro al tuo grembo ho vita.   14

82.

Oh regal roof of mine, this divine place,[70]
once sea of pleasure for me, now of grief,
joy then — while I could feel my lord's embrace,
pain now — as my cruel fate would have, cruel thief.   4
    Where, strolling with my love, time's flight was brief,
oh, flourishing, delightful garden space,
I clamor, cry, in crying leitmotif,
which Echo will, from nearby cave, retrace.   8
    These richly adorned rooms and halls ornate,
reflect only my horror and my fright;
I pine there with an ill incurable.   11
    Oh, when will this harsh dolor terminate?
No change of place, or time, by day, by night,
will make my mourning more endurable.   14

83.

Oh sweet and dearest home of mine, Tifernum,[71]
wherein I spent most happy my best years;
therein brief was the joy, but long the tears,
for dark and bitter night eclipsed my Sun.   4
    In you, with him I lived; now a mean urn
his heart encloses, and my heart with his,
nor do I hope for respite from my lays,[72]
and, languishing, my soul of death does learn.   8
    My turbid mind, intellect troublesome,
were succored by Apollo's tutelage,[73]
with which I tempered cruelest Fortune's rage.   11
    And if, when life has turned its final page,
my relics, urn, you will with his inhume,
I'll say that, dead, I have life in your womb.[74]   14

---

[70]The Bufalini castle at San Giustino.
[71]The old Roman name for Città di Castello, where Giulio Bufalini had built a town palace and where Francesca preferred to live.
[72]Lays, medieval poems, here used as poems of lamentation.
[73]Apollo, the god of poetry and protector of the Muses.
[74]The urn's womb.

84.

Compare this sonnet to Petrarch's *Vago augelletto che cantando vai* (*Rime*, CCCLIII). His *verresti in grembo* (line 7) becomes *vienmi in grembo* (line 6), and his feminine *quella cui tu piangi è forse in vita* (line 10), becomes *Forse colui, per cui sì dolce piangi, / è in vita* (lines 9–10). There is also Bembo's *Solingo augello, se piangendo vai* (*Rime*, XLVIII), which could be another influence, where besides *lai* we also find the concept that the bird will perhaps find his companion: *Ma tu la tua forse oggi troverai* (line 5).

> Vago augellin, cui in sì dogliosi lai
> tra folti rami dolce pianger odo,
> che fai, ch'in versi anch'io la lingua snodo,
> benché 'n stil rauco e disuguale assai.   4
>   Deh, lascia 'l nido, ove solingo stai,
> e vienmi in grembo, e mi dimostra il modo
> del tuo tremulo stil, ch' udir sì godo,
> e cantiam ambo i trapassati guai.   8
>   Forse colui, per cui sì dolce piangi,
> è in vita, e udendo i tuoi pietosi accenti,
> verrà, ché più da te non si scompagni.   11
>   Ma io speme non ho che i miei tormenti
> tregua abbian mai, me ch'ognor più mi lagni
> ch'in tutto il mio bel Sole i raggi ha spenti.   14

85.

> Diletto mio, che 'l sol mi rassomigli,
> e quanto bello sei, tanto fedele,
> ché non rispondi e stai così crudele,
> e qual solevi già non mi consigli?   4
>   Non vedi tu con quai feroci artigli
> squarcia Fortuna del desio le vele?
> Forse tu desto al suon di mie querele
> a soccorrer venisti i miei perigli?   8
>   Ben riconosco le sembianze e gli occhi
> del mio signore, la bell'aria umana,
> e l'ardente desio fa che ti tocchi.   11
>   Lassa, ma pesco il sen d'un ombra vana
> e dico fra pensier torbidi e sciocchi:
> misera, di dolor voi farti insana?   14

84.

Oh pretty bird, whom sweetly I hear plying,
among lush leaves, crying with such sad lays,
to utter verse, I, too, with tongue, am trying,
in stuttering style, unlike yours in all ways.   4
    Oh, leave your lonely nest now, would you, please?
Hop in my lap, and show me, edifying,
your trembling tones which, hearing, I so praise;
let's sing in unison, our grief allying.   8
    And maybe he for whom your sweet cry's meant
is still alive, and at your loving accent,
never to stray, will at your side alight.   11
    From my affliction, though, I've no respite.
I have no hope, and ever more lament,
for my beautiful Sun all light has spent.   14

85.

Oh you, twin of the sun and my delight,
as equal to its glow and just as true,
why won't you speak? Why stand so stiff and tight?
Why will you not advise me, as you do?   4
    Are you not wakened by my loud complaint?
Are not those beastly claws within your view?
Will you not move to remedy my plight
as Fortune shreds desire's sails in two?   8
    Well do I recognize the looks, the eyes,
the noble, human bearing of my sire;
I touch him then, stirred by my passion's fire.   11
    Alas, I fetch the breast of hollow shade,[75]
admonish so my troubled thoughts, unwise:
"Oh, wretched one, does sorrow drive you mad?"   14

---

[75]The author is addressing a portrait of her husband and is carried away by her longing for him.

86.

Linfe, ch'al pianger mio cresciute siete,
che fuor del letto in copia or'inondate,
i miei lamenti al suon vostro accordate,
mentre tranquille e limpide correte.   4
    Se sì rapido e leve il corso avete,
che da la vista mia vi dileguate,
perché 'l mio duol, con voi, via non portate
e nel fondo del mar no'l sommergete?   8
    L'empio mio fato no'l consente, ond'io
vivo senza sperar d'aver mai pace,
poiché senza rimedio è 'l penar mio.   11
    Ogni altra gioia al cor sentir dispiace,
e sol qualche conforto è, al dolor rio,
spiegare in versi il mal che mi disface.   14

87.

Mentre il sol gira l'emisfero intorno,
va 'l bifolco il suo campo inculto arando,
né fatiga, né gel, né ardor curando,
pur si riposa al tramontar del giorno.   4
    Grave remo altri spinge e fa ritorno
col braccio al sen, che 'l legno ir fa volando,
le stanche membra al fin riposa, quando
veleggian l'aure in placido soggiorno.   8
    Ma di mia vita a l'aspra e lunga guerra
non giovano i pensier, vane son l'opre,
ché mai pace trovar non posso in terra.   11
    Così talor procella urta e ricopre
nave che in alto mar s'aggira ed erra,
per cui lume nel ciel mai non si scopre.   14

86.

Waters, with my ample tears bestrewn,
and swelled beyond your banks that overflow,
while with your tranquil clarity you go,
will you to your sound my laments attune?   4
    When from my view you're out of sight so soon,
why not take my grief with you, all my woe
to sea, to drown in deepest undertow,
as ever light and rapid is your run?   8
    She will not grant my wish, cruel Destiny,
thus must I live devoid of hope of peace,
as for grief there remains no remedy.   11
    So any joys touching my heart displease,
but for harsh pain one consolation stays:
explain in verse the sorrow that destroys me.   14

87.

While sun the sphere revolves within its realm,
the peasant plows uncultivated farm;
though heat, cold and fatigue put him to test,
nevertheless, at end of day, he'll rest.   4
    A heavy oar a man[76] pulls to his breast,
thrusts out and back to make the boat go fast;
at day's end he, too, rests his weary arm,
when breeze will sail him to a place of calm.   8
    But for my life of long and jarring turmoil,
thoughts do no good, and useless, too, is toil,
for there's no peace on earth that I might ponder; 11
    just as a storm would jolt and cause to founder
a ship that wanders lost as high seas roil,
while in the sky no light guides to firm soil.   14

---

[76]A man rowing a boat.

88.

Carchi di neve i' veggio i colli intorno,
il piano, i poggi, il monte e l'Appenino,
orrido fatto ogni più bel giardino
e brevissimo a noi splendere il giorno.   4
    Il sol non scalda, e tardi a noi ritorno
fa con l'aurato raggio mattutino;
non canta e sta nascosto ogni augellino;
al cristal fan le gelid'onde scorno.   8
    Sì del mio cor sparito è 'l bel sereno
ché, poiché del mio Sol sparvero i rai,
inverno di dolor fatto è 'l mio seno.   11
    E de le Muse invece ond'io cantai,
questo ciel, queste valli ho ingombro e pieno
di pianti, di sospir, d'amari lai.   14

89.

Aspri monti, antri opachi, ombrosi boschi,
ove in su l'età verde a brun vestita,
menai piangendo solitaria vita,
or oltre l'Alpe, or tra i paesi toschi.   4
    A voi, fra i miei pensier gravosi e foschi,
narrando, chiesi al mio gran duolo aita,
e del mio genitor l'aspra partita
piansi, e temprai del cor gli amari toschi.   8
    Lunge da voi congiunta al caro sposo,
trar lieta i dì sperai ne'miei riposi,
fra lieti abitator de la cittade.   11
    Morte s'oppose ai miei desir gioiosi,
ché lui mi tolse, ond'or, lassa, m'accade
che io rieda ai monti, agli antri, ai boschi ombrosi.   14

88.

I see the hills about burdened with snow,
the valley, knolls, the mount and Apennines;
turned horrible is lovely gardens' glow,
while day for us just only briefly shines.　　　　4
　　The sun brings us no heat, and late will show,
albeit with gold rays at morning-time;
birds do not sing, and stay incognito;
the frozen waves shame all things crystalline.　　　　8
　　Just so, my heart did lose its air serene,
when my Sun disappeared with all its rays;
my breast's become a winter full of pain.　　　　11
　　Where Muses once I'd laud in sweet refrain,
I now load sky and valley with a bane
of tears, of sighs, and of my bitter lays.　　　　14

89.

Rugged mountains, dark caves, forest's shade,
where, during my green years[77] and dressed in brown,[78]
a solitary life, in tears, I led,
you lie past hills and many a Tuscan town.[79]　　　　4
　　My grievous, darkest thoughts to you I said;
the harsh death of my father I did mourn;
for my great grief, I asked of you your aid,
thus bitterest heart-poison I laid down.　　　　8
　　Far from you and conjoined with my dear spouse,
happy, I hoped to lead days of repose,
here in this town[80] with people ever glad.　　　　11
　　My joyous wishes Death would then oppose,
and snatch him up, alas! Now thoughts arouse,
recall you, caves and mountains, forest's glade.　　　　14

---

[77]Her youth.
[78]A plain brown dress was worn by working women. See poem **14**.
[79]The poet is recalling the wild environment of Gattara where she grew up.
[80]The town of Città di Castello.

90.

Antri diletti, care piante ombrose,
rivi, siete que' voi chiari e correnti,
che v'accordaste al suon de' miei lamenti,
mentr'io non tenni le mie pene ascose?   4
    Echi, siete que' voi cui mie dogliose
note ridir udìa con tronchi accenti?
Prati e que' voi sì lieti e sì ridenti,
ove il seno m'empìa di gigli e rose?   8
    Voi que' vaghi augellin, che l'armonia
dolce snodaste, mentre stava a l'ombra
tessendo i fior, temprando il dolor rio?   11
    Sazia del mondo a voi mi pongo in via,
poiché il peso mortal tanto m'ingombra,
ché con voi pace avrò servendo Dio.   14

91.

Libero e picciol Borgo, ove nodrita,
orfana, ahi sorte, fui da' miei primi anni,
ove col latte incominciar gli affanni
che punto poi non fer da me partita.   4
    O stanza, o solitudine gradita,
spesso a voi del pensier dispiego i vanni,
sperando al mio dolor con questi inganni
dar qualche posa, e a l'affannata vita.   8
    Or vagheggio l'ameno, e or l'alpestre,
or le selve, or i prati, or gli aspri monti,
ove talor cacciai fera silvestre.   11
    Ora giacer mi sembra in riva ai fonti,
ora il canto ascoltar d'augel campestre
finché de la mia vita il dì tramonti.   14

90.

Are you the same, my brooks and currents clear,
to whom my hidden pain I would lay bare,
attuning to the sound of my laments,
and you, delightful caves, dear, shady plants?   4
 Echoes, do I hear your old accents,
truncated words, repeat to my sad plaints?
And meadows, you so happy and so fair,
whose lilies, roses on my breast I'd wear?   8
 And lovely, little birds, did you unfurl
sweet harmonies for me while, in the shade,
to temper pain, garlands of flowers I'd braid?   11
 I'm on my way to you, tired of the world,
and heavy by my mortal burden weighed,
for with you peace I'll find while serving God.   14

91.

Small and free *borgo*[81] in which I was fed,
where with my milk my suffering began,
and pain that never left my side again,
from my first year, by fate an orphan made.   4
 Oh room, and just as welcome solitude,[82]
there unto you my thoughts most often run,
where I hope for repose in fond illusion
from my afflicted life, my saddened mood.   8
 I yearn, at times, for that scene, now alpine,
now pleasant, of those woods and peaks and plain,
where I once hunted beasts throughout the wilds.   11
 At times, I seem to rest and to divine,
while lying by a brook, a bird's refrain,
as my last day of life sets past the hills.   14

---

[81]It is not clear whether *borgo* (village) is used in the sense of a small place, or for Borgo Sansepolcro, where Francesca was born. But since she refers to herself as an orphan, she must mean Gattara, her uncle's castle, which clearly is the subject of the rest of the poem, and which was called "free Cathay" in poem **1**.
[82]The author's room in her uncle's castle at Gattara.

92.

Caro, giocondo mio paese tosco
dove menai la mia fiorita etade,
e dove largo il Ciel di sua bontade,
sposo mi diè, da cui tal don conosco.   4
    L'antico nido ben riconosco,
in cui godei l'amata libertade,
per que' giardin, per quelle amene strade,
dolce cantando al seren aere, al fosco.   8
    Ahi, quante volte poi che fui disgiunta
dal mio signor, t'ho lagrimato in vano,
fuor di te di dolore a morte giunta.   11
    Ma se 'l corpo da te stassi lontano,
a te men vivo col pensier congiunta,
questa sembra al mio duol medica mano.   14

93.

Stanza, dove le luci apersi al pianto
il dì de l'infelice nascer mio,
se ben per breve spazio il fato rio
mi ti concesse ai genitori acanto,   4
    ché te lasciai rivolta in negro manto.
A rivederti spingemi il desio,
ancor ch'io pensi a la cagion perché io
fui da te lungi, ne sospiro in tanto.   8
    E ben riveggio voi, mura dilette,
ma non in voi le glorie e gli splendori,
che vi aportava il padre e i frati miei.   11
    E pur un non so che vien che mi alette,
a rimembrar coi vostri antichi odori
quel sospirato ben ch'io non godei.   14

92.

Dear, joyful, Tuscan land of mine,
my bloom of youth was spent here years ago,
where Heaven, then most generous and kind,
gave me my greatest gift, my spouse, I know.   4
    My old home[83] is so well-known to my mind,
the cherished freedom that it did bestow,
to roam the garden and the roads that wind,
while sweetly singing to sky's gloom or glow.   8
    Oh, many times when distance would command
my lord from me, I'd cry for you in vain,
then parted from you, too, near death from pain.   11
    But if, in body, far away I stand,
in thought, joined to you always I remain,
which seems to grant my grief a healing hand.   14

93.

Oh room,[84] in which my eyes opened to tears,
upon my birth, that day unfortunate,
a gift you were to me, my parents near,
although brief respite from my cruel fate,   4
    as wrapped in black cloth I'd soon leave their gate.
Desire to see you again takes me here,
but if what kept me back I contemplate,
the memory will sigh upon sigh stir.   8
    I see and recognize you, my dear walls,
but not the glory in you, or the splendor
my brothers brought to you, as did my father.   11
    And yet, a something vague here does enthrall,
with your familiar odors, to recall
the joy I never had, that good most longed-for.   14

---

[83]Her uncle's castle at Gattara.
[84]The room in which the author was born. This poem seems to describe an actual visit to her paternal house, where her brothers were still living.

94.

Per l'erba del giardin fiorita e cara,
con lenti passi vo 'l mio duol temprando,
or voi, chiusi cespugli, ricercando,
or siedo presso d'una fonte chiara.   4
    Col suon de l'onde la mia pena amara
accordo, e in versi vo 'l mio duol sfogando,
or per l'ombrose selve intorno errando,
e così il cor da Morte si ripara.   8
    Ed or, quando la notte il mondo imbruna,
e 'l velo azurro suo scopre sì bello,
vo mirando le stelle ad una ad una.   11
    E vagheggio fra lor or questo, or quello
chiaro segno del Ciel, così men dura
fo la mia pena e 'l mio mortal flagello.   14

95.

Aure, che così dolci mormorando
gite fra l'ombre de le piante amene,
ove dimoro e a disfogar mie pene
solinga i giorni miei ne vo menando.   4
    Tenere erbette, in cui m'assido quando
vo tessendo di fior varie catene;
limpide linfe, e voi, minute arene,
con cui le doglie mie vo numerando,   8
    dite voi, quanti sono i miei lamenti,
e le lacrime sparse, onde irrigate
siete da questi lassi occhi dolenti.   11
    E voi, romite mie selve beate,
e voi, soavi armoniosi venti,
fate fè del mio duol, voi lo spiegate!   14

94.

Amidst the garden's precious, floral grass,
at times to find you, bushes closely set,
at times beside a fountain clear, to sit,
with laden steps I go to quell distress.   4
    At times, I seek the shade of forest path,
or with the sound of waves my bitter curse
I harmonize, and vent my pain in verse,
so that my heart might shelter take from Death.   8
    And now, when earth is darkened by the night,
whose lovely veil of blue I see emerge,
then, one by one, I look upon the stars;   11
    now here, now there, among them near and far,
a heavenly, clear sign informs my sight,
and lightens my ordeal, my mortal scourge.   14

95.

Sweet breezes, where you murmur as you wend
amidst the shade of many a lovely plant,
there do I go when often I must vent
my grief, as all alone my days I spend.   4
    And tender blades of grass, on which I sit
while twining flowers in a garland's strand;
clear waters, and you, tiny grains of sand,
with whom I number all my countless plaints;   8
    you must proclaim how many are the sighs
and tears I shed, with which your waters crest,
from these most wretched, soulful, weeping eyes.   11
    And you, my woods, with solitude so blest,
and you, my gentle winds harmonious,
spread my grief on your wings, and testify!   14

96.

Ah, se perduto ho, lassa, ogni mio bene
ché di goderlo fu sì breve l'ora,
perché non perdo la memoria ancora,
per far men gravi le mie dure pene?   4
    Ah, ché pur sempre il cor fisso ritiene
quel desio che qual fiamma arde e divora,
e m'è più duro a sofferir che allora
che di vederlo il cor pascea di spene?   8
    Se m'hai tolto, empio fato, il mio diletto,
il mio sposo, il mio ben, la mia speranza,
deh, trammi ancor l'imago sua dal petto,   11
    ché questo poco viver che m'avanza,
pace abbia e ponga in Dio tutto l'affetto,
ché vano è 'l pianger mio, la rimembranza.   14

97.

O primavera, sì vezzosa e bella,
pur ogni anno tornar ti veggio a noi,
ma teco altro tornar non veggio io poi,
che del perduto ben mia doglia fella.   4
    Che giova ch'abbia in questa parte e 'n quella,
ameni campi e machine d'eroi,
s'ogni rara beltà vien che m'annoi,
senza la fida mia propizia stella.   8
    Dopo la pioggia il ciel si rasserena,
si placa 'l mar dop' orrida tempesta,
sol fissa e immota ognor sta la mia pena.   11
    La rosa spiega al sol la ricca vesta,
i gigli, i fior, la terra è d'amor piena,
ogni cosa per me sola è funesta.   14

96.

Oh, if I've lost, alas, all happiness,
enjoyed for what seemed to me a brief hour,
why don't I lose, as well, memory's power,
to lessen my grief's weight and my distress?   4
    Why is my heart so fixedly obsessed
on that desire, a flame that burns, devours,
more difficult to endure than before,
when hope of seeing him nourished my breast?   8
    Cruel fate, since you have my delight erased,
my spouse, my love, my hope, at very least
smite from my soul his image too, I pray,   11
    so that the bit of life I've left will be
enjoyed in peace, with God my passion placed,
for vain are tears, and needless memory.   14

97.

Oh springtime green, so charming and so fair,
I see you return to us every year;
with your return I see, though, and must bear
lost joy which brings me ferocious despair.   4
    What good does it do for me that there are
delightful fields and heroes here galore,
if all rarefied beauty is a bore
without my faithful and propitious star?   8
    The sky returns serene after the rain;
horrid storm passed, the sea calms down again;
my grief alone stays firm and motionless.   11
    The rose, in sun, displays her regal dress;
earth, buds and lilies all are amorous;
for me alone, each thing elicits pain.   14

98.

Grate ombre sparse in questi ameni colli,
or tra le piante ed or nei prati erbosi,
dove sento gli augei garrir vezzosi,
movo solinga il piè con gli occhi molli.   4
    Con voi, Parche, di star non mi satolli,
ché par che con le Muse in voi riposi
e d'Elicona i fonti preziosi
faccian l'acque spruzzar per più rampolli.   8
    Tosto a volo s'inalza l'intelletto,
ed or con alti carmi, or con sommessi,
disacerbo 'l dolor, c'ho dentro il petto.   11
    Per voi rinunzio ogni più ricco tetto,
e 'n voi più tosto di fermare elessi
la mia stanza, il mio nido, e 'l mio ricetto.   14

99.

Ahi, dolorosa vista. Occhi miei lassi,
riconoscete voi lo sposo amato,
quel già sì augusto aspetto, or sì cangiato:
disteso in questi, ohimè, gelidi sassi?   4
    Femmi Amor, lassa, a lor volgere i passi
a veder quel che m'è da lor celato,
e 'l grave duol del suo dolente fato,
bagna or col pianto mio quest'antri bassi.   8
    Caro mio ben, in questo chiuso speco
stai tu, che con mirabil ornamento
machine ergesti agli alti monti eguali.   11
    Quando fia ch'io mi riunisca teco
per terminar le mie sciagure e i mali,
poiché ne porta ogni mia speme il vento?   14

98.

Dispersed throughout these lovely hills, kind shadows,
wherein I hear birds chirp with charming cry,
with you I walk alone, with tearful eye,
now among plants, now over grassy close.   4
    I do not tire of being with you, Parcae,[85]
for with you and the Muses there's repose,
where Helicon,[86] its fountains ever precious
in flowing jets spurt waters to the sky.   8
    At once, on wing, my intellect will rise;
with songs sublime or those in subtle guise
I mollify the hurt that fills my breast.   11
    For you, I do renounce the richest house;
to make my chamber in you I have chose;
in you, I'll build my shelter and my nest.   14

99.

Oh, woeful sight.[87] Oh, my poor, weeping eyes,
that noble cast of his, once so well-known,
so transformed, lying under this cold stone,
do you my cherished spouse now recognize?   4
    Alas, it was my love that made me turn
to see within this tomb what, hiding, lies;
and my great pain about his sad demise
calls forth my tears to bathe this low cavern.   8
    Oh my dear love, inside this narrow cave
you rest, you who with bold initiative
built great works to high peaks equal in kind.   11
    When will I with you my communion have,
to end my woes and my misfortunes grave,
since all my hope is scattered on the wind?   14

---

[85]The three goddesses who presided over the birth, life and death of mankind.
[86]Mountain in Greece, home to the Muses.
[87]Poems **99** and **100** were written when Giulio Bufalini's tomb was opened in order to enlarge it into a family crypt. Note that the author makes no macabre descriptions.

100.

Quest' è la man, amato mio signore,
che sì dolce e cortese a me porgesti,
e del santo imeneo lieta stringesti
il dolce laccio, che m'avinse il core?   4
    Son questi gli occhi, ohimè, dal cui splendore
prendeva lume, or chiusi atri e funesti?
Quest' è la cara bocca onde mi desti
così dolci ricordi a tutte l'ore?   8
    Queste le braccia, che con tal dolcezza
al tuo ritorno mi gettavi al collo,
cadenti, a me cagion d'aspra amarezza?   11
    Ahi, che tal è 'l mio duol che dir non pollo
mia lingua; o Morte, or or mio stame spezza,
ond' abbia a lato a lui l'ultimo crollo.   14

101.

Caro mio ben, che in questa angusta fossa
giaci, e pur già con l'ampia tua ricchezza
fabriche ergesti di sì gran bellezza
quanto architetto mai dissegnar possa.   4
    Le mie volendo a le tue nobil ossa
unir, condotta già ne la vecchiezza,
tanto accresiuta ho sua primiera ampiezza,
che la prosapia e noi ricever possa.   8
    Non mi rest' altro ormai, che prender porto
dopo sì lunga e perigliosa guerra,
qui dove tu ne stai gelido e morto.   11
    L'alma al Ciel vada, ove ogni ben si serra
a trovar per pietade in Dio conforto,
e fra la terra tua questa mia terra.   14

100.

Oh, my belovèd lord, is this the hand[88]
you offered me, so gentle and so courtly,
encircling my heart within a band
which bound me, glad, in holy matrimony?   4
      Are these the eyes, alas, whose rays splendidly
gave me light, now closed, dark and moribund?
And is this the dear mouth with which you made me
sweet keepsakes that I prayed might never end?   8
      Are these the arms that, with such sweet finesse,
you threw around my neck at your return,
and when removed, brought me bitter distress?   11
      A grief so great, my tongue cannot express;
oh Death, of my life's fabric break the yarn,
so at his side I'll take my final rest.   14

101.

Belovèd, whom this grave does now confine
in narrow space[89] yet with your riches vast,
you built such edifices in the past,
an architect might aspire to design.   4
      So to unite your noble bones with mine,
since I may to myself assign old age,
this place I have decided to enlarge;
our progeny with us it will enshrine.   8
      Nothing remains for me but to touch shore,
after so long and perilous a war,
with you where you reside here, dead and cold.   11
      To Heaven may my soul, with good secure,
go find, through mercy, comfort there in God,
and with your dust let them my dust inter.   14

---

[88]See note to preceding poem.
[89]Poem written after the completion of the Bufalini Chapel in the church of Sant'Agostino in Città di Castello. Note that Francesca addresses her dead husband to explain why she had the work done.

102.

S'io volgo gli occhi a voi, dolci miei figli,
ogni affanno e dolor temprando andate,
voi, cari pegni, il fin sperar mi fate
di così fatigosi aspri perigli.   4
 Né potran far d'invidia i fieri artigli,
ch'io con voi sempre, e voi meco non siate,
care del mio signor reliquie amate,
per voi non vuo' cangiar sorte e consigli.   8
 Viver voglio io con voi, con voi morire,
patir per amor vostro, alme a me care,
di Fortuna crudel gli sdegni e l'ire .   11
 Se a più forti anni io voi veggia arrivare,
fra le dolci speranze io prendo ardire
di trovar posa a le mie pene amare.   14

103.

Or ch'il mar de le cure, amato figlio,
benché turbato, solcaremo insieme,
sicura è la mia nave e più non teme
di Cariddi e di Scilla il gran periglio.   4
 Perché tu a me l'aita, io a te 'l consiglio
porgerò ognor che l'onda avara freme,
e così varcherem le rive estreme,
con lieto core e con sereno ciglio.   8
 E come in te femmi avanzar l'amore
il nome di colui ch' amai cotanto,
mio, mentre piacque al Ciel, sposo e signore,   11
 così la luce, in sì funebre ammanto,
riveder speran gli occhi, e insiem 'l core
di prender posto in questo Egeo di pianto.   14

102.

Sweet children,[90] when I have you here with me,
all of my grief and pain you mitigate.
Dear keepsakes, you give me the hope to see
an end to perils harsh, immoderate.   4
    Never will envy, with its claws ferocious,
part me from you; we will together be
always, my lord's belovèd vestiges;
for you, I'll have no change of destiny.   8
    I'll live with you, die with you, this I presage;
for you alone, souls dear to me, I'll bear
the brunt of Fortune's cruel contempt and rage.   11
    To find a pause to bitter pain I'll dare,
in this true hope, to keep you with me near,
so I will see you reach a stronger age.   14

103.

Belovèd son,[91] now that this sea of care,
though stormy, we will here together sail,[92]
though Scylla and Charybdis[93] promise peril,
my ship secure, I will no longer fear.   4
    For you'll give aid to me, I to you counsel,
and so to the far shores will we draw near,
with calm and happy hearts and with eyes clear,
when greedy wave rages to bode us ill.   8
    And since, in you, my love doubled in scope,
by name of him, whom my heart did revere,
my spouse and lord, however brief the years,[94]   11
    though I am cloaked in black and mournful cope,
my eyes again seek light, my heart has hope
to take a place within this sea of tears.[95]   14

---

[90]The Italian *figli* translates as both "children" and "sons."
[91]Written for Giulio, her firstborn son, as the author indicates in the printed text of her *Rime*. He had obviously reached an age of maturity so as to be seen by his mother as a support.
[92]We will share responsibilities.
[93]A dangerous whirlpool in the Strait of Messina (between mainland Italy and Sicily), fatal to many a ship. Charybdis was on the Sicilian shore, Scylla on the opposite.
[94]Her son was given his father's name and Francesca mentions it so she can declare her love for her husband.
[95]Metaphor for life and death.

104.

Oggi Ottavio, il mio dolce pargoletto,
chiude duo lustri, ond'a ragion debb'io
grazie d'un tanto don render a Dio,
ch'ei scema il duol del vedovil mio letto.   4
    Io benedico con materno affetto
quante volte gli ho porto il latte mio,
coi baci tempro in lui quell'aspro e rio
dolor, che già mi avrebbe aperto il petto.   8
    Cresci, e 'l valor e lo splendor rinova
sì come il nome del gentil germano,
e questo sprone a più virtù ti mova.   11
    So ben, che 'l mio sperar non sarà vano,
poi che col suo valor gareggi a prova
ne l'opra de l'ingegno e de la mano.   14

105.

L'angel che Dio ti diè per tuo custode
allor che gli occhi apristi a questa luce,
sia difesa, o figlio, e sia tuo duce
che ti sottragga ognor da l'altrui frode.   4
    Ei ti segni la via ch'a vera lode
il cristiano guerrier guida e conduce,
la via che de la gloria anco riluce
del padre tuo, ch'in Ciel beato or gode.   8
    Tu ministro di Dio, cui solo ascrivo,
s'egli, ch'amai, che desiai cotanto,
ad onta di Fortuna è fin qui vivo,   11
    or, ch' ha di te maggior bisogno, quanto
e forse più d'ogni soccorso privo,
deh, per pietà non gli ti tôr da canto.   14

104.

Today, my little one, Ottavio,[96]
is ten years old, and rightly must I send
thanks unto God for this gift of a son
who palliates the pained bed of a widow.   4
    With love maternal do I bless so often
the many times I offered him my milk,
and kisses I bestow on him to slake
my hurt, which would by now rip my heart open.   8
    Grow then, and so renew the prowess, splendor
of your most noble brother and namesake;
thus spurred, even more merit may you take.   11
    And it is not in vain that I so speak,
for you compete already with his valor
in deeds of intellect and those of armor.   14

105.

The guardian angel given you by God,
when your eyes this, the light of earth, espied,
let him be your defense, oh son, your guide[97]
so to protect you from other men's fraud.   4
    The right way let him unto you confide,
by which a Christian knight gains true applause,
the way that shines still with the deeds we laud
of father, who in Heaven does reside.   8
    Oh minister of God, to you I make
this plea, that he whom I have loved so long,
despite cruel fate, is still alive and strong,   11
    now with this danger he must undertake,
bereft of all support, his life at stake,
please do not leave his side, for pity's sake.   14

---

[96]Ottavio was born in 1582, so this poem was written in 1592 for his tenth birthday. His "namesake" was his half-brother, Giulio Bufalini's son from his first marriage, who died as a soldier.

[97]Addressed to her son, Ottavio, who is about to depart for war for the first time. The author implores protection for him from his guardian angel. Note that she addresses first her son, and then the angel, line 9. The "he" in line 10 refers to Ottavio.

106.

Campion di Dio, che fusti già diffesa,
contro empio drago, di real donzella,
se pur anche ti cale il far più bella
forse e più dubbia e perigliosa impresa,   4
     ecco pugna per Dio, per la sua chiesa,
il mio figlio in età sì tenerella,
in quell'età ch'altri agli scherzi appella,
tu seco sia, che non riceva offesa.   8
     Ché molto è fero d'oriente il drago,
e del suo proprio onor molto è il mio figlio,
e de l'onor di Dio bramoso e vago.   11
     Ma che puote un fanciul senza consiglio?
Sol con l'aita tua già 'l cor presago,
invitto il vede uscir d'ogni periglio.   14

107.

Vergine pia, per quell'ardente amore
che tu portavi al tuo figliuol diletto,
quando tra scherzi ti suggea dal petto
il puro latte, liquefatto il core.   4
     E per quel che soffristi, aspro dolore,
quando in croce ei pendea vile e negletto;
e s'ha in mio pro il tuo gaudio e il tuo diletto
de l'amor e del duol forza maggiore,   8
     ti prego, alta Regina, umilmente,
che 'l generoso figlio a me difenda
da barbara ed a te nemica gente.   11
     Per te fa tu che vincitor si renda,
che meco viva e di pio sdegno ardente
del proprio sangue in onor tuo più spenda.   14

106.

Oh champion of God, who did defend
against an evil dragon, princess fair,[98]
if you would like a chance at deed more rare,
at more perilous foe your hand to lend,   4
    see now, my son for God and church contends,
at so tender an age, fights without peer,
an age when others still play without care;
stay with him, let no danger him offend.   8
    For most ferocious is the Eastern dragon,
and of his honor very proud my son,
and for God's honor, eager to take arms.   11
    What can a mere boy do, deprived of counsel?
Yet, with your help, my heart may fear dispel;
I'll see him home unconquered, out of harm.   14

107.

For such a burning love, oh Virgin[99] pious,
for that belovèd Son You did adore,
when at Your breast He fed, felicitous,
of Your pure milk, Your liquefied heart pure.   4
    And for that bitter sorrow that You bore,
when He was hung, abandoned, on the cross;
if bliss and love's delight be in my favor,
if Your love over pain has greater force,   8
    most humbly do I beg You, highest Queen,
that You protect my fearless son for me,
from people barbarous, Your enemy.   11
    For Your sake, speed him home, in victory,
so with a burning and pious disdain
of his own blood, for You, he'll bleed again.   14

---

[98]The author, in her motherly fear, invokes St. George to protect Ottavio, who is leaving for war at a very tender age.

[99]Having first implored his guardian angel, then St. George, Francesca now implores the Mother of God to protect Ottavio and bring him back alive so he can fight again in the future.

108.

Note the alternative rhyme in the *quartine*: ABBA/BAAB.

Quando sarà quel lieto giorno, quella
ora da me sì desiata, ch'io
ti veggia, o figlio, o parte del cor mio,
ed oda il dolce suon di tua favella?   4
     Perché, se fiumi tu del sangue rio
spargi per Dio di gente a lui ribella,
a sparger fiumi queste luci appella
de la tua vita e del tuo ben desio.   8
     Né cosa alcuna mai mi racconsola,
fuor ch'il saper che per te pugna il Cielo,
e questa al cor viva speranza è sola.   11
     Viva, diss' io, ché puro, ardente zelo
fa cotal forza al Cielo ch'ancor invola
a le fiamme l'ardore, il freddo al gelo.   14

109.

Note the alternative rhyme in the *quartine*: ABAB/BABA.

O vista, sì gran tempo desiata
che m'ha gli occhi equalmente al cor contento,
mentre del figlio mio novella grata
attendo, il veggio, odo il suo dolce accento.   4
     A l'improvisa gioia il cor mi sento
palpitar di dolcezza inusitata,
vola il desio per lui baciar, ma lento
va il piè, sì la virtù resta adombrata.   8
     Pur tanto può l'amor che mi trasporta,
che gli mi getto avidamente al collo,
non so ben dal gioir se viva o morta.   11
     Io miro e di mostrar non mi satollo
l'affetto ch'il materno amor comporta,
così del fondo del dolor m'estollo.   14

108.

The hour I now anticipate so well,
that happy day I pray we both shall reach,
when I will hear the sweet sound of your speech,
oh son, of my heart's own material.　　　　　　4
　　Rivers of blood in God's name you dispatch,
rebellious blood of wicked infidel;
parallel rivers heartache does compel
from eyes that seek your welfare, and beseech.　　8
　　No consolation on earth will suffice,
but knowing Heaven will take up your part,
the one and burning hope left to my heart.　　11
　　Burning, I say, for faith pure, passionate,
bids Heaven to dispel with equal force
and miracle, heat from flame, cold from ice.　　14

109.

Oh vision I so desperately longed for,
as I awaited good news of my son,
sight to my heart and eyes alike reviver,
I see him, hear his dulcet voice's tone.[100]　　4
　　At joy so sudden, my heart, overcome,
pulses with happiness not much felt prior;
alas, my feet are slow and I go numb,
to kiss him surging in me great desire.　　8
　　The love I hold for him spurs me ahead,
with arms around his neck, my embrace flies;
I know not if, for joy, I'm live or dead.　　11
　　I gaze at him and show, unlimited,
the love a heart maternal does comprise;
I feel myself from wells of grief arise.　　14

---

[100]Poem written for the unexpected return of Ottavio.

110.

Note that line 13 is hypermetric, for it has an extra syllable.

Gli alti edifici, ai tuoi pensier uguali,
che cominciasti, amato mio signore,
sperai finir per tuo, per mio splendore,
ma furon vani i miei disegni e frali,   4
    ché rio fato m'ha posto in tanti mali,
ché con l'aver m'ha dissipato il core,
né cessa ancor dal solito furore
di saettarmi con gli acuti strali.   8
    E discordie e litigi e morbo e morte,
veder m'ha fatto ne l'amata prole,
e pur respiro in sì contraria sorte.   11
    Ma fa pur quanto vuoi, se ben mi dole,
ché in paradiso fatt'ho più degno e forte
nido, e tema non ho che lo mi invole.   14

111.

Note the alternative rhyme in the *quartine*: ABAB/BABA.

Misera anima mia, posar dovresti,
benché 'l tuo mal sia così acerbo e forte,
poiché dal nascer tuo, lassa, vedesti
che t'aportava il mondo iniqua sorte.   4
    Quando de' cari genitor la Morte
privandoti, meschina, i dì traesti
fuor delle ricche tue paterne porte,
né i consueti amor de' tuoi godesti,   8
    dovea bastarti, né del mondo al mare
infido entrar, ma ben sposarti a Dio
che suol le spose sue di gioia ornare.   11
    Non saria il tuo sperar gito in oblio,
né sentiresti al cor pene sì amare,
che crescer più non pon nel petto mio.   14

110.

Those buildings tall and broad, as was your vision,
that you initiated, my dear lord,
I'd finish for our splendor, with accord,
but paltry, frail and vain has been my mission.[101]   4
    For Fate assailed me with such foul condition,
my heart's been dissipated by wealth's hoard;
to fell me with her darts, sharp as a sword,
her anger has not ceased, or ammunition.   8
    And disagreements, quarrels, sickness, death,
she made me witness in each cherished son,
yet in my adverse state, I linger on.   11
    Though it pains me, do as you feel you ought.
In Paradise, my noble nest is done;
that you will wrest it from me, I fear not.   14

111.

Oh my poor soul, you know you ought to rest,
although you feel a pain so sharp and great;
the world offered to you a lot unjust
since birth, alas, my poor unfortunate.   4
    For Death, to take both parents, did not wait,
and hence you led, poor girl, a life so tossed,
beyond the trust of rich, paternal gate,
where all familial love to you was lost.   8
    Not quite enough, the sea, perfidious,
of this cruel world you swam; instead, as spouse
of God,[102] you'd have known joy, as His consort.   11
    And thus, your hope would not have been forgot,
nor would you house such bitterness of heart,
that in my breast can't grow to more excess.   14

---

[101]Addressing her husband, Francesca complains that she was unable to complete his building projects, because of the quarrels among their sons as to how their money should be spent. There was no harmony in her family.

[102]Because of her sons' quarrels, Francesca states that it would have been better for her to have chosen the convent rather than marriage.

112.

Tornerò, lassa, al mio paterno tetto,
di cui, per agradir fraterno amore,
priva mi resi, ond' or piango l'errore,
senza il germano e fuor del mio ricetto?   4
    Starò dove lo sposo mio diletto
lassomi, s'empio fato il suo furore
mi volge e spoglia d'ogni pace il core,
ché abandonare il nido è il piè costretto?   8
    Che farò, lassa? Dove avrò riparo?
Avrà mai fine il precipizio mio?
Struggerommi mai sempre in pianto amaro?   11
    Soccorso altro per me non è che Iddio.
Il mio ricorso a te, Signor, sia caro,
che tu sei degli afflitti il Padre pio.   14

113.

I figli no, ma tu, Signor, sei quello.
Conosco io ben che con rigor cotanto
sei venuto ver me sotto il lor manto,
e m'hai posto in sì duro, aspro flagello.   4
    Non per far del mio cor strage e macello,
ma per camparlo da l'eterno pianto,
ch'era in amarli, ohimè, fisso cotanto
che sì avea il vero amor fatto ribello.   8
    Ma qual pietoso Padre, a' miei perigli
porto hai la santa onnipotente mano,
ch'ho il serpe scorto fra le rose e i gigli.   11
    Scorgo ch' è ogni altro amor fallace e vano,
onde, destando in me saggi consigli,
quasi da serpi andrò da lor lontano.   14

112.

Shall I return, then, to my father's house,[103]
which, for my brothers' love, I left, and yet
this error I do solemnly regret:
no brothers and no home, and at a loss?   4
    Shall I remain where my belovèd spouse
bequeathed, if Fate her fury does impart,
to route again all peace from out my heart,
constrain me to abandon home by force?   8
    Alas, what shall I do? Where seek accord?
Is there no end to this steep precipice?
Will I forever weep remorseful tears?   11
    For me, there is no refuge but in God.
Let my recourse to You, my Lord, be dear,
oh You, to the afflicted, Father pious.   14

113.

Not sons of mine, oh Lord, no, it was You,
who with such rigor, I now realize,
visited me while hidden in their guise,
and sent me scourge as such I never knew.   4
    My heart You would not massacre, eschew,
but save from grief and eternal demise,
for fixed on loving them so were my eyes,
my heart turned rebel to Your love more true.   8
    Like Father merciful, You gave Your hand
to me in need, and just, omnipotent,
the snake midst rose and lily made me see.   11
    All other love I now know fraudulent.
Hence, roused by wise advice, I understand:
I will from them,[104] as from a serpent, flee.   14

---

[103]Poem written after Francesca was pressured by her sons to yield the administration of their possessions to them. She found it impossible to live with them, but she could not return to her paternal house. She departed Città di Castello for Rome and found refuge in the Colonna household.
[104]Her sons.

114.

Quando l'acerba nova il cor m'afflisse,
figlio, che rea di te giunse improviso,
non l'oso dir. Restommi il cor conquiso
e non so dove l'alma allor sen gisse.   4
    E perché il male in ben si convertisse,
con lacrime mi affissi al paradiso,
fin che pietosa a me rivolse il viso
quella che Dio per noi bear n'ascrisse.   8
    O gran Madre di Dio, Madre diletta,
a me la vita e libertate al figlio
desti, pur ch'ero ad impetrar sì intenta;   11
      fammi intera la grazia, a te si aspetta,
tronca i litigi e leva il duro esiglio,
ché se poi moro, allor morrò contenta.   14

115.

O sommo Iddio, pur a pietà commosso
t'han le lagrime mie, l'ardente prece,
ché 'l ghiaccio a un guardo tuo si liquefece,
che era in quei cor sì congelato e grosso.   4
    Per mio ben m'hai con tal flagel percosso,
ché d'odio e di guerra or segue invece
amore e pace; tua potenza fece
miracolo tal, che tal chiamar lo posso.   8
    Or se per le discordie fui costretta,
disperata, pigliar dal nido il volo,
l'union per tua man mi vi rimetta.   11
    La gioia è al par del sostenuto duolo:
l'anima in pace di morir aspetta
e ne l'opera tua mi riconsolo.   14

114.

How much the painful news about you, son,
I dare not tell, I shall not give it voice,
of how it pierced my heart, how it did stun,
and what befell my soul, I can't surmise.[105]   4
    And so that evil would to goodness turn,
with tears I fixed my gaze on Paradise,
till, merciful, Her face showed me concern,
the one whom God ordained that we rejoice.   8
    Oh great Mother of God, Mother of all,
You freed my son, and gave me back my life,
for my entreaty to You, so intent;   11
       please make Your grace, Your favor to me, whole;
repeal my exile[106] and truncate their strife,
for should I die, I then will die content.   14

115.

In mercy for my tears and ardent prayers,
oh God so great, Your forces did converge,
for in those hearts[107] the ice, so gelid, huge,
melted to naught at just one look of Yours.   4
    For my own good, You sent me such a scourge,
but now I've love and peace, not hate and wars;
a miracle was wrought here by Your powers,
that by no other name would it be judged.   8
    If, desperate from their discord uncontrolled,
I took flight from my home, now by Your hand
in their reunion, send me back again.   11
    My joy is equal to my endured pain,
and I will die in peace, as it was planned,
for in this deed of Yours I am consoled.   14

---

[105] At the news that Ottavio was arrested, in 1615, after he unlawfully occupied, with armed men, the Bufalini castle at San Giustino while Giulio was away. The poem was written after Ottavio's liberation from prison.
[106] From Rome.
[107] In the hearts of her sons who were quarreling. The poem was written upon the news that her sons had made peace, which Francesca took as a miracle.

116.

Se tante amare lagrime e sospiri
sparso avea ne l'età mia tenerella,
perché con nuovo turbine e procella
giù ne l'abisso del dolor mi tiri?   4
    E con tal sdegno contro me ti adiri,
Morte crudel, d'ogni pietà ribella,
che d'una inaspettata e ria novella
inacerbi per sempre i miei martiri!   8
    Mi togliesti il mio ben, l'amato figlio,
e quel colpo mortal che lui trafisse
mi piagò il sen d'irreparabil male;   11
    e vivo, e spiro per divin consiglio,
ché se per Morte il mio languir finisse,
saria dolcezza il colpo suo fatale.   14

117.

Quando, figlio, pensai che i gravi affanni,
nel corso di mia vita sopportati,
fosser per mezzo tuo rasserenati,
Morte t'uccise sul fiorir de gli anni.   4
    Ahi, chi fia che sanar possa i miei danni,
se con la morte tua son raddoppiati?
Perverse stelle e ingiuriosi fati,
avess'io di seguirti almeno i vanni,   8
    poscia che star in sì contraria sorte,
vita non è, ma un sempre mai languire,
duro assai più ch'a sostener la morte.   11
    Ma se il penar al Ciel ne fa salire,
fammi, Signor, sì paziente e forte
che le vestigia tue possa seguire.   14

116.

If plenty were the bitter sighs and tears
I shed throughout my early, tender years,
why now, with this new whirlwind, tempest thus
hurl me again so far down pain's abyss?   4
    and with such scorn direct at me your wrath,
rebel to all compassion, oh cruel Death,
for, with such unexpected, horrid news,
my harsh life you continue to abuse!   8
    My dear, belovèd son[108] from me you rent,
and with that mortal blow to him, so fierce,
with ceaseless pain my own breast you did pierce,   11
    yet I live on and breathe by God's intent.
Ah, Death, if you would only end my torment,
your fatal blow to me would be but bliss.   14

117.

    Just when, my son, the great pain that I knew,
which you alone would finally placate,
grave hurt that in my harsh life I'd accrue,
to kill you in your prime,[109] Death did not wait.   4
    Oh, who could ever my ills mitigate,
as, with your death, they double and renew?
My stars perverse, my injurious fate;
if only I had wings to follow you.[110]   8
    For being dealt this lot[111] in life adverse
is languish eternal, no life at all,
more difficult by far than death to take.   11
    But if my pain will earn me Heaven's call,
oh Lord, make me strong, patient, for this sake:
Your footsteps You'll allow me to traverse.   14

---

[108]The poem was written for the death, in 1623, of Ottavio, which is also the subject of sonnets **117–19**.
[109]Ottavio died at the age of 40–41.
[110]You = Ottavio.
[111]Francesca's destiny.

118.

Compare this poem with sonnet **50**, written for the birth of Giulio, which also starts out with *Viscere del mio sen*. There is another parallel construction in the imaginary response in the first case of the baby, that cannot speak as yet (*madre, gradisco un tanto amore*, line 13), and here (lines 9–11), as if pronounced by the dead son, Ottavio. Note the alternative rhyme in the *quartine*: ABAB/BABA.

Viscere del mio sen, figlio diletto,
figlio di duol, tu notte e dì mi stai
fisso nel cor, anzi tu l'hai dal petto
rapito e teco 'l porti ovunque vai.   4
   Né spero, ahi lassa, riaverti mai,
né più conforto e refrigerio aspetto,
e freddo, e muto, e con trafitti rai
parmi vederti entro il funereo letto.   8
   Or sembri dirmi: "madre mia, ti lasso,
come in vita mi amasti or dopo morte
di me ti caglia e ne l'estremo passo."   11
   E pur non è che 'l viver mio si scorte,
di ferro è questo sen, fatto è di sasso,
ché resta integro a un duol sì grave e forte.   14

119.

Quel grand' animo tuo, d'onor, di gloria,
che vivendo, figliuol, mai sempre avesti,
or in morte in oblio non già ponesti
qual sempre degno di famosa istoria.   4
   E dei passati error festi memoria,
e gli occhi e il cor nel Redentor ponesti,
con zelo tal ch'a le parole e ai gesti
mostrasti del nemico aver vittoria: 8
   non curando il morir, mostrando solo,
dei mal spesi anni in servitù del mondo,
pentimento, tristezza, affanno e duolo.   11
   E te n' gisti con Dio, lieto e giocondo,
ché in ciò pensando sol mi racconsolo,
ché nel mar del dolor non mi profondo.   14

118.

Fruit of my womb,[112] my son, belovèd so,
son of my grief, day, night, you're with me, fixed
inside my heart; nay, from my breast instead,
my heart you've snatched, and it goes where you go.   4
    Nor do I hope to once again have you,
for cold and mute and with your eyes transfixed,
you fill my mind, in your funereal bed.
No comfort or relief is there in view.   8
    You seem to say: "Mother, my leave I take.
As you loved me in life, now, with my death,
until your death, your love for me evoke."   11
    My life is not undone. I yet have breath.
Cast iron is my breast, solid as rock;
at harm so grave, so fast, it will not break.   14

119.

You'd not forsake, when death your life did claim,
the great spirit for honor, glory won,
that you displayed throughout your life, my son,[113]
behaving true to self, worthy of fame.   4
    You summoned to your memory past sin,
to your Redeemer turned your soul and aim,
and with such zeal your acts and deeds did name,
that victory from final foe you'd win.   8
    For death, a disregard you always had;
for years wasted to worldly cares incurred,
regret, affliction, pain and heart so sad.   11
    With God you did depart, jocund and glad,
and I console myself, when this I ponder,
so in my sea of sorrow I'll not founder.   14

---

[112]These same words were used in poem **50**, written for the birth of Giulio, not Ottavio, while here they are used for Ottavio. Another stylistic parallel between these two poems is the imagined address of the son to his mother, in both cases impossible, for one was a baby, the other was dead.

[113]Ottavio. This poem comments on his Christian death.

120.

Quando ti vidi, unico mio, partire,
così oppresso dal mal ch'a pena in piede
stavi, tanto il dolor prese in me sede
che mi sentia dal sen l'anima uscire.   4
    Ed a pena potei le labbra aprire
quando ch' umil mi t'inchinasti al piede.
Ti benedissi, ti baciai, ti diede
l'alma il suo "val," ti seguitò il desire.   8
    E se 'l corpo restò doglioso e mesto
con gli occhi molli, teco venne il core
a' tuoi bisogni ognor vigile e desto.   11
    E se mai grazia avrò vederti fuore
di questo mal, de la mia vita il resto
trarrò pur lieta, infin a l'ultim' ora.   14

121.

Morte, che pensi far, Morte crudele?
Lo sposo e il figlio, qual tempesta il fiore,
m'hai tolto, e svelto m'hai dal petto il core,
ond'io spargo ad ognor pianti e querele.   4
    Ch'or mi prepari nuovo assenzio e fele,
torva mirando anco il figliol maggiore.
Deh, muoviti a pietà del mio dolore,
né de la speme mia troncar le vele.   8
    Depon la falce tua, tempra lo sdegno.
Sovvengati di tanti pargoletti
e della miserabil mia vecchiezza: 11
    questa tronca del fil, condotta al segno.
Ché badi? Il tuo venir ché non affretti?
E lassa lui nella viril fortezza.   14

120.

Such hurt lodged itself deep within my heart,
my only one,[114] as you parted from me,
by illness weighed and bowed, tentatively,
that from my breast I felt my soul depart.   4
    When at my feet you humbly bent your knee,
hardly could I then move my lips apart;
I blessed you, kissed you, that my soul impart
adieu, as my love trailed your destiny.   8
    But though my body stayed, sad and in pain,
tearful my eyes, my heart followed you on,
always alert, vigilant to your need.   11
    And if I will at last favor obtain
to see you safe, a happy life I'll lead
till my days' end, till my last breath I've drawn.   14

121.

Death, cruel Death, what are you up to now?
My spouse, my son, as storm ravages flower,
you ruined, and my heart from breast you tore,
that tears, laments, from me forever pour.   4
    To my affliction, oh, some mercy show,
as new bitterness, poison, you prepare
by menacingly eyeing my one heir;
do not sever the sails from my hope's prow.   8
    Put down your scythe and temper your disdain;
remember on whom all our babes depend,
that my unhappy life draws near its end.   11
    Sever my thread; my mark of time is past.
Why do you hesitate? Why not make haste?
And let him, in his manly prime, remain.   14

---

[114]Giulio, who was now Francesca's only remaining son, fell gravely ill after his brother's death and came to seek his mother's blessing.

122.

Pargoletto gentil, reliquie belle
de le viscere mie, del figlio amato,
poiché di tanto ben m'ha Dio privato,
con farmi oggetto a le contrarie stelle.   4
 Tu plachi del mio cor l'aspre procelle
che 'l gran mar del dolor produce irato,
o per mio refrigerio al mondo nato,
vivi e tempra il martir che 'l cor mi svelle.   8
 Ché quel vivace spirto e 'l chiaro ingegno
che mostri in verd' età, spero con gli anni
di veder giunto di virtude al segno.   11
 Così vai riparando ai comun danni,
e gemendo e sperando mi sostegno,
se per Morte non termino gli affanni.   14

123.

O mio dolce conforto, idol diletto,
del mio cor luce e de le mie pupille.
Come le stelle il cielo, a mille a mille,
fregian le grazie il tuo gentil aspetto.   4
 Amoroso bambin, puro angeletto,
fai che d'amor mi sfaccia e mi distille,
qualor con quelle luci alme e tranquille,
dolce mi vedi e mi ti stringi al petto,   8
 e quella bocca, anzi animata rosa,
m'accosti e dai quegli amorosi baci
ch' hanno del cielo ogni dolcezza ascosa.   11
 Cresci ed i grandi tuoi spirti vivaci
crescan con gli anni, ond'io qual son bramosa,
colmo ti veggia poi d'onor veraci.   14

122.

Dear gentle, little one,[115] and remnant fair
of my own womb, of my belovèd son,
whom God soon took from me, a blessing gone,
exposing me to my contrary star.   4
    You placate all my heart's storm of despair
which sorrow's sea, when swelled with rage, does spawn;
you, to this world for my great solace born,
live on, soothe over my heart's telling scar.   8
    Your lively temperament, intellect clear,
which show at your green age, with every year
I hope will carry you to valor's height.   11
    Our common loss continue to repair;
hope will sustain me, as I cry outright,
if Death does not my pain first terminate.   14

123.

Delightful solace, sweet idol of mine,
the light both of my heart and of my eyes,[116]
as stars by thousands beautify the skies,
the graces so adorn your gentle mien.   4
    Pure little angel, baby amorous,
you make me melt, dissolve from love so fine,
when with your eyes divine, calm and serene,
you take me in and to my breast you press.   8
    That mouth of yours, an animated rose —
draw near, give me your loving kisses, those
which all of Heaven's sweetness therein hide.   11
    Grow now, let the vivacious soul you chose
grow with the years, so I, with love and pride,
may see you brim with honor bona fide.   14

---

[115]This poem, addressed to Ottavio's son, Giovanni Battista, was written shortly after his father's death in 1623. Ottavio married in 1617, so Giovanni Battista must have been born in 1618, for in summer 1619 he took his first steps (as described in a letter by his father). He followed a military career and died in 1670. The Bufalini family continued from his descendants.

[116]Addressed to her grandson Giovanni, born in 1612, son to Giulio. Francesca expresses her grandmotherly love with exuberance. Note that poems **123–25** were written years apart for two of Giulio's sons. They are placed here together for the theme of grandmotherly love and pride.

124.

Fra tutti i cavalier nel giostrar usi,
molle garzon, sei vincitor rimasto
e con popolar grido ed alto fasto,
sì che non sa l'invidia onde ti accusi.   4
  Faticar con virtù non mai ricusi,
con qual si voglia marzial contrasto,
ma con invitto core, animo vasto,
opri e fai gli altri attoniti e confusi.   8
  E se col fior ci dai maturi e belli
frutti, come di te sperar debb'io
che 'n sua stagion sian l'opre tue preclare?   11
  Degli avi lo splendor tu rinovelli;
vivi, ardito campion del germe mio,
e fa' le glorie tue sempre più chiare.   14

125.

Fiero in uno e leggiadro in sella assiso,
venisti in giostra, o Bufalin garzone,
non qual nuovo guerrier, ma qual campione
che faccia ogni altro rimaner conquiso.   4
  Quinci la gloria ai tuoi grandi atti arriso,
empì di spessi plausi il lungo agone,
e, meditando a te palme e corone,
pendea da la tua lancia il popol fiso.   8
  Or, se nel cominciar dato hai tal saggio
del nativo, magnanimo tuo core,
che sarà nel seguir del bel viaggio?   11
  Segui e cresci con gli anni il tuo valore,
che questo, dato a noi, sia picciol raggio
appo quel che darai del tuo splendore.   14

124.

Of all the jousting knights used to the game,
you, my tender boy,[117] remain the victor,
with high display, to popular acclaim,
depriving envy of any detractor.   4
    Never do you refuse to strive with valor
with any tool of war you choose to aim;
you go attack, stun, confuse every other
with your unconquered heart, spirit untamed.   8
    If, in your flowering age, you give us fruits
lovely, mature, what will I see from you
in season's prime, from your most noble impact?   11
    The splendor of your ancestors renew —
oh, thrive, you ardent champion of my roots,
and take even more glory for your acts!   14

125.

Proud, yet lightly on the saddle prone,
you came to joust, oh Bufalini boy,[118]
with an intent to vanquish foe that day;
not fighter green but as a champion.   4
    And your great deeds were favored there with glory:
the long arena with applause rang on;
anticipating then your palms and crown,[119]
fixed so upon your lance was every eye.   8
    If, as beginner, this be sample only
of your heart's innate, generous way,
what bodes for the remainder of your journey?[120] 11
    May years expand your valor as contender,
that this day be, for us, just one small ray,
compared to how you'll shine in all your splendor. 14

---

[117]Written for grandson Nicolò (1611–1676), son to Giulio, when he won his first joust in Città di Castello. He spent his military career in France, married twice, but left no sons.
[118]Written for the same grandson of poem **123**, this time for his first tournament. He, too, spent his military career in France and died there in 1647.
[119]Symbols of victory.
[120]Journey of life.

126.

Del laberinto uman, cieca alma mia,
t'incresce uscir, che sì dubiosa stai?
Deh, su meschina, a che indugiando vai?
Prendi il sentier de la diritta via.   4
     Non vedi quanto il tuo pensier travia
dal Ciel, ed ognor più crescono i guai,
e sempre vivi in dolorosi lai,
né rimedio per te par che vi sia?   8
     Se perduto hai con gli anni ogni speranza
di trovar pace e cresce ognor la guerra,
questo almen breve viver, che t'avanza,   11
     spendilo in Dio, sollevati da terra,
ché lui servendo, ti darà possanza
di viver là, dov' ogni ben si serra.   14

127.

Ahi, come presto via siete fuggiti,
verd' anni miei, mal conosciuti giorni,
quand' erano i diletti e i miei soggiorni
fra canti e suoni, in luoghi ermi e romiti.   4
     Di questo umano Egeo fremere i liti
non avea inteso, e sue procelle e scorni,
ma nei prati e giardin di fior adorni,
menava i giorni miei dolci e graditi.   8
     Tempo sereno, età fiorita e cara,
in cui gli egri pensier m'eran lontano,
sciolta dal giogo di sì gravi affanni.   11
     Lassa, or la vita m'è noiosa, amara,
e si raddoppia il mio penar con gli anni,
ch' ha sol Morte al mio mal medica mano.   14

126.

Oh my blind soul, why do you linger, sorry
to quit the human labyrinth today?
Oh, courage, miserable one, why tarry?
Take the straight path, finally, the right way.   4
  From Heaven your thoughts have gone so astray,
with painful lays you lament constantly,
do you not see? Only your troubles stay,
nor is there for you any remedy.   8
  If, with the years, your hope to find repose
you've lost, to see just increase of your strife,
at least what's left to you of your short life,   11
  spend it with God, from earth rise up, transposed,
for, serving Him, He'll grant you strength so rife
to live therein, where all good is enclosed.   14

127.

How swiftly, now I see, you've sped away,
my verdant years, my unacknowledged hours,
when with delight, on remote paths, I'd stray,
to sing and play midst solitary bowers.[121]   4
  I'd not yet felt the tremor of the shores,
the storms and scorn, of sorrow's human sea,
but in gardens and glen adorned with flowers,
I'd spend my sweet, hermetic days, carefree.   8
  A blooming age, a time serene, a land
where painful thoughts were far away from me,
when, from the yoke of sorrow, I could flee.   11
  I now live life, alas, so bitterly,
and with my years my troubles so expand,
just Death will give my ills a healing hand.   14

---

[121]Francesca recalls with nostalgia her youth and her carefree life at Gattara.

128.

Ahi, ché non sorge più l'usata vena
che mi solea racconsolar sovente?
Perché l'afflitta e nubilosa mente
sempre di liti e d'aspre angustie è piena.   4
    Dopo la pioggia suol tornar serena
l'aria, ch'era sì fosca, e 'l sol lucente,
ma, lassa, in me non torna mai ridente
il torbido pensier, l'aspra mia pena.   8
    Se 'l desir in Parnaso a gir m'alletta,
m'è 'mpedito il camin da più contrasti,
ch'a dietro mi fan gir con maggior fretta.   11
    Potrò mai tanto riparar che basti?
Quando la via non mi sarà interdetta,
e non fia più che a' miei desir contrasti?   14

129.

Ecco, boschi, ch'io torno a rivedervi,
care mie piante, solitari monti,
antri remoti e cristallini fonti,
per trovar in voi pace e per godervi,   4
    e per mia stanza e per delizie avervi,
benché a l'occaso il giorno mio tramonti,
ché da varcare al Ciel voi siete ponti,
per fugir l'acque immonde e più non bervi.   8
    L'ambizione in voi non ha ricetto,
onde struggonsi ognor gli egri mortali:
da voi lungi è la frode e 'l rio sospetto.   11
    Qui senza intoppo a Dio si spiega l'ali,
onde l'alma, gustando il ver diletto,
sprezza gli altri piacer caduchi e frali.   14

128.

Oh, why will the same vein flow there no longer
that many times ran through me to console?
Affliction does my cloudy mind control
and fills me full of quarrel, stress and anger.[122]   4
    After the rain, serene returns the air
once ominous; the sun restores its glow.
Alas, my atmosphere does still bestow
more gloomy thoughts and bitterest despair.   8
    If to Parnassus' gates desire calls me,
I find the road by sundry contrasts closed,
and with great haste to turn back I am chidden.   11
    Will ever I escape, as my needs be?
When will the way no longer be forbidden
and no one to my wishes be opposed?[123]   14

129.

My dear plants and most solitary mounts,
my caves remote and my crystalline founts,
my forests, returned to you here am I,
to find my peace with you, of you enjoy,   4
    to flee the waters[124] foul, drink not one ounce,
to take shelter within you, to ensconce,
though my day sets as to me death draws nigh,
for you are bridges up to Heaven's sky.   8
    Destroying mortals, a thing called ambition
does not reside in you, does not assail;
far from you stays all fraud, evil suspicion.   11
    To God I'll spread my wings here without fail;
my soul, soaring to truest elevation,
will scorn other delight, fleeting and frail.   14

---

[122]The author laments the impossibility of dedicating herself to poetry, because her mind is overwhelmed with affliction.

[123]An allusion to the harsh words that her son, Giulio, sometimes directed at her poetic endeavors.

[124]Waters of life.

130.

Querce antiche, o duri cerri, o faggi,
alteri pini e verdeggianti abeti,
ove a menar i dì tranquilli e lieti,
son giunta in questi lochi ermi e selvaggi.   4
    Qui faranno i pensier dritti viaggi
al Ciel e in Dio staran fissi e quieti;
qui svelar suol gli arcani più secreti
il divin lume con gl'immensi raggi.   8
    Chi non vorria fuggir l'aspre procelle
di questo Egeo di vita, e in voi far stanza
per gustar di là su cose sì belle?   11
    Qui dolce, sopra ogni mortal usanza,
cantan gli augelli, in queste parti e in quelle,
onde ebra, l'alma ne l'orar s'avanza.   14

131.

Note the alternative rhyme in the *quartine*: ABAB/BABA.

Vaneggiante pensier, ch' errando vai,
la notte e 'l dì senza aver mai quiete,
quanto più volgi in te gli andati guai,
tanto entri più ne la terrena rete.   4
    Deh, cessa omai, tornin tranquille e liete
le Muse, e rasserena i mesti rai,
e tutti caggian, ne l'oblio di Lete,
i duri affanni e non risorgan mai.   8
    Va in Paradiso e nel Castalio fonte
bevi e rischiara l'offuscato ingegno,
e con nobil opra dispensa l'ore.   11
    E se non giungi al desiato segno,
dove le voglie son bramose e pronte,
basta che lieto renda il tristo core.   14

130.

I've come to your wild places solitary,
oh ancient oaks, and acorns that endure,
oh beeches, and proud pines and verdant fir,
happy to lead in peace each, every day.   4
    My thoughts will straight to Heaven go from here,
and, fixed on God, will be at rest, will stay;
herein His divine light, with immense ray,
is wont to show His secrets most obscure.   8
    Who would not choose to flee the savage storm
of this harsh sea of life, shelter in you,
to enjoy from up here the things most true?   11
    Here, sweet to me beyond all human custom
sing the small birds, through trees and meadow rue,
that my enraptured soul may prayer pursue.   14

131.

Delirious thought, you go, disorganized,
night and day, wander back, forth, restlessly;
the more you ponder past hurt, to excise,
the more caught up you'll be in this net earthly.[125]   4
    Let Muses return to you, calm and happy,
and make serene again your mournful eyes,
and let fall to oblivion in Lethe
all your affliction, never more to rise.   8
    Go, drink of Paradise's Castalian spring[126]
and clear your intellect, now become dim;
allot your hours to a true, noble thing.   11
    And if you do not reach the longed-for aim,
though you be so desirous, ready, thirsting,
it is enough you've made your sad heart sing.   14

---

[125] Although addressed to her "thought," the author is talking to herself.
[126] A spring in the Parnassus mountain, consecrated to the Muses and Apollo.

132.

Or che sorge nel ciel la vaga Aurora
e sparge i gigli e le vermiglie rose,
e sì vaghe, e sì belle, e sì pompose,
ch'i campi intorno e i verdi prati infiora, 4
    sento gli augei, ch'al susurrar de l'ôra
fra i folti rami e fra le siepi ombrose,
con le vezzose lor note amorose,
par che dican: "su, su, ché fai dimora? 8
    Vedi il ciel com' è bello, e vedi il sole
che ad aggiornar il mondo ormai s'appresta
e pone ai suoi destrier la briglia e 'l morso? 11
    Volgi a Dio gli occhi, il core e le parole,
e dal suo divin lume oggi mai desta
attendi da sua mano alto soccorso." 14

133.

Veggio i capelli d'or farsi d'argento,
e perder quasi ogni vaghezza il volto,
ma non lasciare il cor, fallace e stolto,
l'ostinato nel mal proponimento. 4
    Anzi più sempre a mortal opre intento,
fra lacci il miro inutilmente avvolto,
giacer nel fango vil tutto sepolto,
e sol trarne in mercè travaglio e stento. 8
    Se cangio 'l crin, se 'l volto, ahi, perché ancora,
misera, non cang'io pensiero e sorte,
né scorgo il fin d'una brevissim' ora? 11
    Ahi, se corro, ahi, se volo oggi alla Morte,
che non tento e non cerco or per allora,
ché non mi sien del Ciel chiuse le porte. 14

132.

Lovely Aurora[127] rises in the sky,
so beautiful, magnificent, so lovely,
scattering lilies and vermilion rose
to blossom in the fields and in green meadows.   4
    In rustling breezes, I hear birds compose,
midst branches thick and shady bushes' close,
in verses amorous which seem to say:
"Arise, arise! Why do you so delay?   8
    Do you not see the gorgeous sky, the Sun[128]
preparing a new day for earth, so bright,
with bit and bridle harnessing his steeds?   11
    Oh, turn to God your eyes, heart, words and deeds;
awake to this day by His divine light,
and from His hand await His benison."   14

133.

I see my golden hair fast turn to white,[129]
and my face almost all its beauty lose,
yet I don't see my silly heart refuse
its unsound plans, or turn less obstinate.   4
    It lies in vilest mud, and out of sight,
ever intent on mortal deeds, obtuse,
and snared uselessly, I see, by the noose,
to add distress and hardship to my plight.   8
    If I change hair and face, and mortal guise,
why do I not, alas, change thought and fate,
or my brief hour's end[130] not recognize?   11
    If it is unto Death my body flies,
I'll not seek Death for now, to tantalize,
for I would not have Heaven shut its gate![131]   14

---

[127]Goddess of dawn.
[128]Apollo, the sun god, rode the sky in his chariot.
[129]Francesca was conscious of the fact that she was aging, but at the same time she was unable to stop lamenting.
[130]My life's end.
[131]The author implies that, as a Christian, she did not seek death, although she hoped for it.

134.

Non pur l'inanellato aureo capello
vedi cangiare il solito colore,
e la faccia apparir qual colto fiore,
che sul nativo stelo era sì bello;   4
    ma volgendo il suo corso alato e snello,
ti fura un dente il Tempo involatore:
messi di Morte son, che l'alma fuore
esca, e tu speri in van farlo novello.   8
    E s'un perduto aver tanto di duole,
misera, che farai, s'in picciol volo
gli altri ti fura il Veglio empio e avaro?   11
    E la vista, e l'udito, e le parole?
Semplicetta, che fai? Raffrena il duolo,
ché vano è contra il Tempo ogni riparo.   14

135.

Note the alternative rhyme in the *quartine*: ABAB/BAAB.

O miserabil uom, che pur formato
fosti per tanti onor dal Fabro eterno,
come sei fatto, ohimè, pel tuo peccato
de la terra e del Ciel obbrobrio e scherno?   4
    Tu fra l'ombre e gli orror del sen materno,
quasi morto e sepolto, anzi che nato
hai tomba anzi la cuna, e, vomitato,
esci poi quindi a soffrir caldo e verno.   8
    Prima che latte altrui, lasso, ti pasce
il proprio pianto, e l'altrui man t'avvezza
ai lacci e a le catene, entro le fasce.   11
    Come fior passa via la giovinezza
tra le cure ed avvien che 'l viver lasce
pria che venghino i dì de la vecchiezza.   14

134.

Not just your curly, lively, golden hair
do you see change its customary color,
your face turn faded as a cut-off flower
that on its living stem once was so fair;   4
 but cutting his swift course, winged avatar,
he steals from you a tooth, Time, that old snatcher;[132]
your soul escapes: Death's messengers these are —
where, futilely, you'd hoped for some repair.   8
 If losing one tooth makes you so complain,
alas, what if, within a minute's reach,
the greedy old man all the rest might snatch?   11
 And what of your two ears, your sight, your speech?
Oh foolish woman, do rein in your pain;
in fighting Time, any defense is vain.   14

135.

By the eternal Maker, wretched man,
for honor vast were you meant to be hewn;
how then did you become, through all your sin,
to earth and Heaven, infamy, buffoon?   4
 In dark and horror of your mother's womb,
before your cradle, yea, before you're born,
you are entombed, as if already gone,
thence, heat and cold to bear, vomited, spew.   8
 Before the taste of milk, poor soul, alas,
you feed on tears, and learn of vassalage,
in swaddling clothes, with snares and chains and cage.   11
 Youth fades like flower amidst the cares that ravage,
and it may be that from this life you pass
so long before the day you reach old age.[133]   14

---

[132]Time was depicted as an old man with wings.
[133]Poem inspired by Marino, who in turn departed from Celio Magno's long composition,
Deus, though the theme appears in the fifteenth century.

136.

A che pur tanto tua mortal figura,
o vanissima donna, or pingi, or fregi,
e ognor l'adorni d'ornamenti egregi,
se quanto è bella più, tanto men dura?   4
    In grembo ad umil sasso, in tomba oscura,
fian chiusi a sera i tuoi superbi fregi,
e tue bellezze e peregrini pregi
fian di putridi vermi atra pastura.   8
    Volgi l'opre e la mente al sommo bene,
e lascia queste transitorie cose
che posto intorno t'han lacci e catene.   11
    Son vaghe e belle in sul mattin le rose,
ma con l'ore, varcato il dì, conviene
restar languenti su le siepi ombrose.   14

137.

Simile a un fiore, a una purpurea rosa,
ch'entro verde giardin sì tenerella
spunta ne l'apparir d'alba novella,
è questa breve vita perigliosa.   4
    Mira, se puoi veder più nobil cosa
ch'ornata, in verde età, donna o donzella,
tant'è leggiadra, amorosetta e bella,
ch'è di vederla ogn' anima bramosa.   8
    Né sì tosto il suo dì giunge a l'occaso,
ch'ogni bellezza sua svanisce e perde,
nè v'è chi più la miri o più la pregi.   11
    O di natura miserabil caso,
che più non si ravviva o si rinverde,
e caggion coi bifolchi ancora i regi.   14

136.

Oh woman vain, why do you, as the norm,
flatter yourself with finest ornament,
paint and accessorize your mortal form;
more beauty gained, less remains permanent.   4
   In darkest tomb, your superb adornment,
at death, a womb of plain stone will inter,
and your rare features, comeliness, be spent
as horrid feed unto the putrid worm.[134]   8
   To highest good, turn time, mind, at all cost,
and leave behind this transitory fare
that will, with noose and chain, only ensnare.   11
   Lovely is every rose in morning's air,
but hours must pass, the day sets, and at last,
on shady bush, each one languishes, lost.   14

137.

To flower similar, to crimson rose,
that, in a garden green in summertime,
sprouts forth as the new dawn begins its climb,
is this our life,[135] so short and perilous.   4
   Nothing more noble, worthy of our praise,
is maid or woman, verdant, in her prime,
so graceful, loving, her beauty sublime,
that, eager, every eye on her must gaze.   8
   But as the sunset lowers on her day,
her beauty fades and vanishes from view,
and no one's gaze, no praise is lost on her.[136]   11
   Oh, this is nature's miserable way;
we don't revive, or stay in bloom forever,
and even kings must die as peasants do.   14

---

[134]Such macabre aspects of death were popular with the Baroque poets.

[135]A common Renaissance theme was to compare a woman to a rose, or stress the short duration of beauty, accompanied by an invitation to love. Francesca goes a step further and compares the two, rose and woman, to life itself.

[136]The author acutely observes that only young and beautiful women are admired.

138.

Fra le potenze a cui soggetti in terra
noi siam, tu la maggior potenza sei,
Morte, ché non perdoni ai boni, ai rei:
giovani e vecchi la tua falce atterra.   4
    Tu fatto hai ritornar polvere e terra
i gran saggi de' Persi, de' Caldei,
gli Alessandri, gli Annibali, i Pompei,
che con te terminaro ogni lor guerra.   8
    Con quanto fasto te ne vai superba
di tante glorie tue, di tante imprese,
ch' hai fatto fin ad or, che far ti appresti.   11
    O Morte dispietata, o Morte acerba,
fin col figlio di Dio gire a le prese
osasti, e vincer parte anco volesti.   14

139.

Queste guance, quest'occhi e questa bocca,
e questa testa tutt' orror, che spenta
miri, misera te, ti rappresenta
la tua, se Morte col suo stral ti tocca.   4
    Anima mia, che o cieca in tutto, o sciocca,
or scorgi, ohimè, quant' al ben far sei lenta,
né 'l tuo stato infelice or ti spaventa.
S'irato or Dio contro te l'arco scocca,   8
    or ch'in difesa tua pur una sola
buon'opra opporre a suo rigor non puoi,
e forse non potrai formar parola.   11
    Deh, cedi dunque al mondo i piacer suoi,
e sol Dio servi, e tosto, ohimè, ché vola
rapido 'l tempo e più non torna a noi.   14

138.

On earth, among the forces that befall
us mortals, Death, you are most powerful,
and neither good nor wicked do you spare,
for, young and old, your scythe fells without care.   4
    To dust and clay you did return them all,
each Alexander, Pompey, Hannibal,
the wisest men of Persia, Chaldea,
who would not cease, but thanks to you, their war.   8
    Proudly you walk, precisely to impress,
with your great acts, each glorious award
you've won, and with those on your future list.   11
    Oh bitter Death, oh Death so pitiless,
you even dared combat the Son of God,
and did on partial victory insist.   14

139.

Regard these cheeks, regard this mouth, these eyes,
this lifeless, horrid head, and you behold,[137]
if Death's arrow should pierce, with touch so cold,
the aspect of your own, your own demise.   4
    My foolish, blinded soul, do realize
how slow you are your good deeds to unfold,
nor is your sorry state by fear made bold.
If God, in anger, aims and arrow plies,   8
    to put up a defense would be absurd,
for not one noble deed could you display,
nor could you say, alas, a single word.   11
    All worldly pleasures to the world transferred,
serve only God; make haste, do not delay,
for time takes wing, and from us flies away.   14

---

[137]The poet is looking at the head of a dead person.

140.

Non hanno altro refugio i miei martiri
che di Florio cantar, parto diletto;
per lui bramo la notte e bramo il letto
chè nuovi carmi a la mia mente inspiri.   4
    Florio, s'anzi ch'io mora i miei desiri
non sortiscano alfin contrario effetto,
celebrar la memoria io ti prometto
de gli amorosi tuoi casti sospiri.   8
    Forse avverrà che dopo irata pioggia
per me sereno il ciel, lucido il sole
torni, e non sempre nubiloso e oscuro.   11
    Vie più che del mio duol m'è grave e duro
che son l'ali tarpate u 'l desir poggia:
pur bisogna voler quel che 'l Ciel vole.   14

141.

Florio mio, tu sei quel che 'n tanti affanni
infino ad or m'hai mantenuto in vita,
ché dal sen fatto avria l'alma partita
per le pene e i martir ch'apportan gli anni.   4
    Al tuo merto tropp' ho deboli i vanni.
È la tua tela di fin oro ordita,
trama non ho sì tersa e man spedita,
che racchiuda il lavor, benché m'affanni.   8
    Ma 'l Ciel per sua mercé, s'ei mai non manca,
veste le braccia mie di nuove piume
ed a tuoi fregi nuovi fregi intesse,   11
    sì spero trarla un dì, dal dubbio franca
e del mio basso ingegno al fosco lume,
pur le grandezze tue saranno espresse.   14

140.[138]

My torments will find no other respite
but Florio to sing, labor's desire;
for him, I long for bed,[139] I pray for night,
so that new verses may my mind inspire.　　　4
　　And if these wishes of mine lose no fight,
my Florio, before I shall expire,
the memory I vow to celebrate
of your chaste sighs, so amorous and pure.　　　8
　　Perhaps for me, after furious rain,
there may return a fair sky, brilliant sun:
the cloudiness and darkness will be gone.　　　11
　　Much heavier to bear than is my pain,
are my clipped wings that carried such ambition;[140]
yet one must kneel before Heaven's volition.　　　14

141.

Florio mine, amid such woe, just you,
for years and to this hour, keep me alive;[141]
my soul would flee, but for you I survive
the grief and pain, crushed by what I've been through.　　　4
　　Though no neat plot, nor quick hand to contrive
have I, to spin your cloth of fine, gold hue,
or polish up the work, still I pursue.
Weak are my wings, but to your merits strive.　　　8
　　Yet Heaven merciful may not take leave,
but with new feathers has my two arms dressed,
and with your beauty, beauties new does weave;　　　11
　　and so I pray, by doubt no longer pressed,
though in dim light, with humble talent blest,
your glory I will truly have expressed.　　　14

---

[138]Sonnets **140** and **141** are taken from Corbucci's transcription of Turini Bufalini's unpublished poems. Both refer to the title's hero of her narrative poem.

[139]The author seeks peace in her bed where, undisturbed, she can dedicate herself to her literary work. She addresses her hero as if he were a person.

[140]Francesca frequently laments that she does not have the proper education needed for writing good poetry; her wings are clipped.

[141]Writing poetry was for the author an escape from life's difficulties and had a healing effect on her.

VIA FOLIOS
A refereed book series dedicated to Italian studies and the culture
of Italian Americans in North America.

Most Recent Titles

RICHARD VETERE
Baroque
Vol. 58, Fiction, $18.00

LEWIS TURCO
La Famiglia/The Family
Vol. 57, Poetry, $12.00

NICK JAMES MILETI
The Unscrupulous
Vol. 56, Humanities, $20.00

PAOLINO ACCOLLA &
NICCOLÒ D'AQUINO
Italici:
An Encounter w/ Bassetti
Vol. 55, Italian Studies, $8.00

GIOSE RIMANELLI
The Three-Legged One
Vol. 54, Fiction, $15.00

CHARLES KLOPP, ED.
Bele Antiche Stòrie
Vol. 53, Italian Cultural Studies, $25.00

JOSEPH RICAPITO
Second Wave
Vol. 52, Poetry, $12.00

GARY R. MORMINO
Italians in Florida
Vol. 51, History, $15.00

Other *VIA* FOLIOS Titles

ADKINS, ET.AL, BRENT: *Shifting Borders*; Vol. 42, Cultural Criticism, $18.00
ANGELUCCI, GIANFRANCO: *Federico F.*; Vol. 50, Fiction, $16.00
BAROLINI, HELEN: *Chiaroscuro: Essays of Identity*; Vol. 11, Essays, $15.00
BAROLINI, HELEN: *More Italian Hours & Other Stories*; Vol. 28, Fiction, $16.00
BELLUSCIO, STEVEN: *Constructing a Bibliography*; Vol. 37, Italian Americana, $15.00
BRIZIO-SKOV, ED., FLAVIA: *Reconstructing Societies in the Aftermath of War*; Vol. 34,
    History/Cultural Studies, $30.00
CANNISTRARO, PHILIP: *Blackshirts*; Vol. 17, History, $12.00
CARNEVALI, EMANUEL W/ DENNIS BARONE, ED. & AFTERWORD: *Furnished Rooms*; Vol. 43, Poetry,
    $14.00
CASEY, ET. AL, JOHN: *Imagining Humanity*; Vol. 25, Interdisciplinary Studies, $18.00
CLEMENTS, ARTHUR L. *The Book of Madness and Love*; Vol. 26, Poetry, $10.00
CONDINI, NED: *Quartettsatz*; Vol. 7, Poetry, $7.00
CORSI, JONE GAILLARD: *Il libretto d'autore, 1860–1930*; Vol. 12, Criticism, $17.00
DEVRIES, RACHEL GUIDO: *Teeny Tiny Tino*; Vol. 47, Children's Literature, $6.00
DIPASQUALE, EMANUEL: *Writing Anew*, Vol. 46, Poetry, $15.00
FAMÀ, MARIA: *Looking for Cover*, Vol. 45, Poetry, $15.00; CD, $6.00
FEINSTEIN, WILEY: *Humility's Deceit: Calvino Reading Ariosto Reading Calvino*; Vol. 3, Criticism,
    $10.00

GARDAPHÈ, FRED L. *Moustache Pete is Dead!* Vol. 13, Oral literature, $10.00

GARDAPHÉ, FRED, PAOLO GIORDANO, AND ANTHONY JULIAN TAMBURRI: *Introducing Italian Americana: Generalities on Literature and Film*; Vol. 40, Criticism $10.00

GIORDANO, ED., PAOLO A. *Joseph Tusiani: Poet, Translator, Humanist*; Vol. 2, Criticism, $25.00

GIOSEFFI, DANIELA: *Blood Autumn / Autunno di sangue*; Vol. 39, Poetry, $15.00/$25.00

GIOSEFFI, DANIELA: *Going On*; Vol. 23, Poetry, $10.00

GIOSEFFI, DANIELA: *Word Wounds and Water Flowers*; Vol. 4, Poetry, $8.00

GRAMSCI, ANTONIO; TRANS. AND INTROD. BY PAOLO VERDICCHIO: *The Southern Question*; Vol. 5, Social Criticism, $5.00

GUIDA, GEORGE: *Low Italian*; Vol. 41, Poetry, $11.00

HOSTERT, ANNA CAMAITI, and ANTHONY JULIAN TAMBURRI, EDS. *Screening Ethnicity*; Vol. 30, Ital. Amer. Culture, $25.00

LAGIER, JENNIFER: *Second Class Citizen*; Vol. 19, Poetry, $8.00

LIMA, ROBERT: *Sardinia • Sardegna*; Vol. 24, Poetry, $10.00

MESSINA, ED., ELIZABETH GIOVANNA: *In Our Own Voices*; Vol. 32, Italian American Studies, $25.00

MISURELLA, FRED: *Lies to Live by*; Vol. 38, Stories, $15.00

MISURELLA, FRED: *Short Time*; Vol. 8, Novella, $7.00

NASI, ED., FRANCO: *Intorno alla Via Emilia*; Vol. 27, Culture, $16.00

PARATI, GABRIELLA, and BEN LAWTON, EDS. *Italian Cultural Studies*; Vol. 29, Essays, $18.00

PASQUALE, EMANUEL DI: *The Silver Lake Love Poems*; Vol. 21, Poetry, $7.00

PICARAZZI, TERESA, and WILEY FEINSTEIN, EDS. *An African Harlequin in Milan*; Vol. 10, Theater/Essays, $15.00

PUGLIESE, STANISLAO G. *Desperate Inscriptions*; Vol. 31, History, $12.00

RICAPITO, JOSEPH: *Florentine Streets and Other Poems*; Vol. 9, Poetry, $9.00

RUSTICHELLI, ED., LUIGI: *Seminario sul racconto*; Vol. 16, Narrativa, $10.00

RUSTICHELLI, ED., LUIGI: *Seminario sulla drammaturgia*; Vol. 14, Theater/Essays, $10.00

STEFANILE, FELIX: *The Country of Absence*; Vol. 18, Poetry, $9.00

TALARICO, ROSS: *The Journey Home*; Vol. 22, Poetry, $12.00

TALARICO, ROSS: *The Reptilian Interludes*; Vol. 48, Poetry, $15.00

TAMBURRI, ED. ET. AL., ANTHONY JULIAN *Italian Cultural Studies 2001*; Vol. 33, Essays, $18.00

TAMBURRI, ED., ANTHONY JULIAN with MARY JO BONA, INTROD. *Fuori: Essays by Italian/American Lesbians and Gay*; Vol. 6, Essays, $10.00

TAMBURRI, ED., ANTHONY JULIAN: *Italian Cultural Studies 2002*; Vol. 36, Essays, $18.00

TURCO, LEWIS: *Shaking the Family Tree*; Vol. 15, Poetry, $9.00

TUSIANI, BEA: *con amore*; Vol. 35, Memoir, $19.00

TUSIANI, JOSEPH: *Ethnicity*; Vol. 20, Selected Poetry, $12.00

VALERIO, ANTHONY: *Tony Cade Bambara's One Sicilian Night*; Vol. 44, Memoir, $10.00

VALERIO, ANTHONY: *The Little Sailor*; Vol. 49, Memoir, $9.00

VISCUSI, ROBERT: *Oration Upon the Most Recent Death of Christopher Columbus*; Vol. 1, Poetry, $3.00

Published by BORDIGHERA, INC., an independently owned not-for-profit scholarly organization that has no legal affiliation to the University of Central Florida or John D. Calandra Italian American Institute, Queens College/CUNY.

Breinigsville, PA USA
02 March 2010
233466BV00002B/3/P